LEARNING DISABILITY

PROBLEMS FACED BY CHILDREN AND STRATEGIES FOR MANAGEMENT

LEARNING DISABILITY

PROBLEMS FACED BY CHILDREN AND STRATEGIES FOR MANAGEMENT

By

Dr. P. Neeraja
Academic Consultant
Department of Home Science
Sri Venkateswara University
Tirupathi (Andhra Pradesh)
(India)

&

Prof. K. Anuradha
Research Guide, Head
Department of Home Science
S.V.College of Sciences
S.V. University
Tirupathi (Andhra Pradesh)
(India)

DPH

DISCOVERY PUBLISHING HOUSE PVT. LTD.
INDIA

Published by:
Namit Wasan
DISCOVERY PUBLISHING HOUSE PVT. LTD.
4383/4B, Ansari Road, Darya Ganj
New Delhi-110 002 (India)
Phone : +91-11-23279245, 43596064-65
Fax : +91-11-23253475
E-mail: discoverypublishinghouse@gmail.com
namitwasan9@gmail.com
sales@discoverypublishinggroup.com
web : www.discoverypublishinggroup.com

First Edition: **2018**

ISBN: 978-93-5056-891-0

Learning Disability:
Problems Faced by Children and Strategies for Management

Printed at:
Infinity Imaging Systems
Delhi

Preface

Learning disability is a hidden problem among school children and causes stress to children, parents and also to the teachers. Children with learning disability will have major adjustment problems in the areas of home, emotional, social and Academic. Special education helps in coping up of problems with LD by giving Individualized Remedial Education Programme. Special education is available for other disabilities like Children with mentally challenged, hearing impairment, visual impairment etc., but very few schools are offering services for children with learning disabilities in Andhra Pradesh state as well as in India also. Hence, there is an urgent need to give attention to this particular aspect.

The present research explored the adjustment problems of children with learning disability in comparison with those children without learning disability. The scope of the study also includes the study of relationship among special education and adjustment problems and also coping up of problems by children with learning disability. Though, research has been conducted on this aspect at abroad, the awareness has been initiated in Indian context recently. Attempt has been made to study the parents' and teachers' perception towards children's adjustments and also coping up by children. The research work will help readers to understand better about learning disability, problems faced by children, parents' and teachers' reactions in understanding the problems and the need of special education which will help children to cope up with the problems related LD.

—**Authors**

Acknowledgements

I take this opportunity to express my deep sense of heartfelt gratitude and devotion to my research supervisor, Dr. K. Anuradha, Professor, Department of Home Science for her meticulous guidance, constant, affectionate care, inspiring discussions and valuable suggestions to complete this work with confidence. I will ever remain grateful to her for her wise counseling and unfailing attention.

My sincere thanks are due to former Heads Prof. D.L. Kusuma and Dr. R.K. Anuradha and present head Dr. K.Anuradha, Department of Home Science, S.V.University for their administrative support.

I acknowledge with sincere thanks the encouragement, helpful comments and valuable suggestions given by Dr. P. Lavanya, Assistant Professor in Statistics, S.V. Agricultural University, Tirupati for her help in statistical analysis of the data.

I owe my profound gratitude and heartfelt thanks to all my subjects of the study, teachers and parents for the kind cooperation in collecting the data and help while collecting the data without which this work could not have been completed.

I express my sincere thanks to DST-INSPIRE, Department of Science and Technology for awarding the INSPIRE Fellowship and for providing financial assistanceduring my Ph.D. course.

I am grateful to my friends Lavanya, Pragathi, Sandya, Mamatha, Nageswari and well wishers amongst the intellectual fraternity who always helped me with their advice, suggestions and encouragement throughout.

I wish to place on record the affectionate help and ambitious encouragement rendered by my parents Sri P.Chenchaiah (Head Master) and P. Padmavathi. I always remember their constant and continues support.

I am grateful to my brother P. Devaraju for his affectionate support and encouragement throughout.

I am at loss of words to describe the forbearance evinced by my husband Mr. K. Rajendra Babu, in making this venture a success. I am indebted for his co-operation and also for his help in typing and proof reading.

In particular, I thank the staff of Sri Prabha Graphics Mr. Krishna and Ms. Mounika for their assistance in typing the thesis work.

— **Neeraja. P**

Contents

List of Abbreviations

ANOVA	–	Analysis of Variance
BP	–	Behavior Problems
BPCL	–	Behavior Problems Check List
CPLD	–	Coping Up of Problems of Learning Disabilities
FSE	–	Full time special education
IQ	–	Intelligence Quotient
LD	–	Learning Disability
LDDI	–	Learning Disabilities Diagnostic Inventory
NA	–	Normal Achievers
NLD	–	Non Learning Disabled
PPERCA	–	Parental Perception of Emotional Reactions towards Children's Adjustments
PRLDS	–	Problems Related to Learning Disability Scale
RS	–	Resource rooms
RSPMT	–	Raven's Standardized Progressive in Matrices Test
SE	–	Special Education
With LD	–	With Learning Disability
With SE	–	With Special Education
Without LD	–	Without Learning Disability
Without SE	–	Without Special Education

1

Introduction

The middle childhood which extends from six to eleven years is crucial stage in children's life during which children enter elementary school. Each period during childhood is marked by basic biological and cognitive changes, as well as changes in the social surroundings where children's daily lives unfold. During elementary school age, children learn about the wider world and master improved athletic abilities, participation in games with rules, more logical thought processes, mastery of basic literacy skills, and advances in self-understanding, morality and friendship (Berk, 2003). Children grasp the concepts of space and time in more logical, practical ways. They gain a better understanding of cause and effect, and of calendar time. At this stage, children are eager to learn and accomplish more complex skills like reading, writing, telling time and so on.

In Piaget's cognitive development stages elementary school age coincides with *'concrete operational stage'*. During this stage children are in pre-adolescent period and try to understand things using logical and concrete reasoning. Children's thinking becomes less egocentric and they are increasingly aware of external events. They begin to realize that one's own thoughts and feelings are unique and may not be shared by others or may not even be part of reality.

In Erickson's psycho-social theory the elementary school age coincides with *'Industry versus Inferiority stage'*. During this stage children begin to attend formal school where they are made to learn various skills and the teachers as well as the school environment generate pressures on them to work harder in order to perform well. Parents also begin to make demands upon the children to lend their hand in household activities. If the child performs well in school, home or in other social environment or is admired for the intellectual pursuits the child will be likely to develop a sense of industry filled with a sense of achievement. On the other hand inferiority develops when negative experiences at home, at school, or with peers lead to feelings of incompetence. Erickson viewed that each stage of life one is faced with a crisis, the resolution of which can have either a good or bad effect on one's adjustment. The failure to master-trust, autonomy, and industrious skills may cause the child to doubt his or her future, leading to shame, guilt, and the experience of defeat and inferiority.

Researchers have supported Erikson's notion that feelings of competence and personal esteem are of central importance for a child's well-being. For instance, children who do not see themselves as competent in academic, social, or other extra-curricular activities during their elementary school years report depression and social isolation more often than their peers.

The transition to formal schooling is a complex and multifarious process that requires simultaneous adjustment processes in emotional, social, behavioural, and cognitive aspects. It involves drastic changes in day structure, behavioural norms, rules, expectations, and demands, in comparison to kindergarten classrooms (Susan, 2006). Disturbingly, empirical evidence shows that 20-30 per cent of children exhibit problems during the first year of school such as difficulty following directions, a lack of academic skills, social skills problems, disruptive behaviour, attention/hyperactivity disorders, anxiety symptoms, and depressive disorders. Extensive research has been conducted over the years to address the diverse needs of children entering elementary school.

Adjustment Problems during Elementary School Age

The development during elementary school age has considerable significance for behaviour pattern and adjustment for later stages. The term 'adjustment' is often used as a synonym for accommodation and adaptation. The term denotes the results of equilibrium, which may be affected by either of these processes (Monroe, 1990). It is used to emphasize the individual's struggle to survive in his or her social and physical environment. The school is the major socialization institution for any child. It is the child's first contact with the world outside the house. During school years a child spends 5 to 7 hours a day in the school. School is one the most important foundation pillars on which the child's personality develops. Children learn proficiencies in various abilities like, learning process and home work, social communications, handling emotion and so on.

Adjustment is a continuous process by which an individual varies in behaviour to produce a more harmonious relationship between oneself and his/her environment. It is a condition in which the behaviour of an individual conforms to the needs of the individual and demands of the environment. In adjustment, both personal and environmental factors work side by side. In adjustment, the two crucial factors are the individual and the environment. In the study of the individual, the considerations are the heredity and biological factors, the psychological factors, and the quality of socialization given to him or her. Whereas, the environment includes all the social factors. Every individual from the time he or she steps out of the family and goes to school makes to a long series of adjustments between the whole unique personality and the environment. The ardent desire of each boy and girl to become an individual person having a healthy physique, a growing intellectual ability, a greater degree of emotional poise and increased participation in social groups, such characteristics enhance one's personality.

During this stage students can engage in problematic behaviours because of health problems, personal or family problems, adjustment or developmental issues (e.g., "immaturity" or self-esteem issues), or general academic difficulties.

Generally behaviour problems are school based and are mainly due to learning difficulty. These problems do not be identified till the child enters formal schooling.

Learning Disability

Learning disability, an unexplained difficulty experienced by children of at least average intelligence in acquiring basic academic skills usually identified during elementary school age.

Learning disabilities generally used as 'LD' is a general term that refers to a heterogeneous group of disorders manifested by significant difficulties in the acquisition and use of listening, speaking, reading, writing, reasoning, or mathematical abilities. These disorders are intrinsic to the individual and presumed to be due to central nervous system dysfunction, and may occur across the lifespan. Problems in self-regulatory behaviours, social perception, and social interaction may exist with learning disabilities but do not by themselves constitute a learning disability.

People with learning disabilities have trouble taking in information through their senses and processing that information accurately to the brain. Usually they will receive scrambling information like a distorted radio signal or fuzzy television picture.

A learning disability is a neurological disorder that affects the brain's ability to receive, process, store, and respond to information. "LD" does not stand for a single disorder. It is a term that refers to a group of disorders.

General learning disability must be differentiated from specific learning difficulty (eg. dyslexia) which means that the person has one difficulty such as in reading, writing or understanding, but has no problem with learning in other areas.

It is interesting to note that many successful people such as Walt Disney, Alexander Graham Bell, and Winston Churchill all had learning disabilities.

Prevalence

Learning Disabilities (LDs) refer to a variety of neurologically-based disorders that affect a person's ability to take in, understand, remember or express information. (Status Canada, 2006).

The prevalence figures can vary widely between states and within a state, depending on the stringency of the method used to determine eligibility.

The prevalence of children with LD is found to be more than any other disabilities in the world. In India children with Learning Disabilities were found to be 10 per cent (NIMH, 2001) among childhood population. According to global literature on LD about 1 per cent of children are born with severe language disability and up to 17 per cent may experience varying levels of language disturbances.

Vijayalakshmi *et al.,*(2011), reported that the prevalence of Learning Disability is at the higher side of previous estimations in India.

Specific Learning Disability affects 5-15 per cent of school going children (Sunil, Rukshana, Madhuri 2011)

Currently, almost 2.9 million school-aged children in the United States are classified as having specific learning disabilities and receive some kind of special education support. In fact, over half of all children who receive special education have a learning disability (24th Annual Report to Congress, 2002). They are approximately 5 per cent of all school-aged children in public schools. (These numbers do not include children in private and religious schools or home-schooled children.) Learning disabilities is by far the largest category of special education.

According to Indian statistics 30-50 per cent of the population has undiagnosed learning disabilities (National Institute for Literacy, 2006).

Dyslexia is widespread with upwards of 15 to 20 per cent of school age children affected.

According to International Dyslexia Association (2006), 80 per cent of the students with learning disabilities have problem in reading. In India also it was reported that 85 per cent of individuals with learning disability have difficulties in the area of reading (National Institute of Child Health and Human Development, 2006).

In 2006 in India it was reported that around 13 to 14 per cent of all school children suffer from learning disorders (National institute of Child Health and Human Development, 2006).

According to the U.S. Center for Disease Control and Prevention (CDC, 2003), 5.3 percent of boys and 3.8 percent of girls ages 5 to 17 were identified as having a learning disability (LD).

The true prevalence of learning disabilities is subject to much dispute because of the lack of a standard definition of LD and the absence of objective diagnostic criteria. Some researchers have argued that the currently recognized 5 per cent prevalence rate is excessive and is based on vague definitions, leading to inaccurate identification. On the other hand, research efforts to identify objective early indicators of LD in basic reading skills have concluded that virtually all children scoring below the 25th percentile on standardized reading tests can meet the criteria for having a reading disorder. While less is known about LD in written expression, researchers estimate its true prevalence at between 8 per cent and 15 per cent of the school population. Research also indicated that approximately 6 per cent of the school population has difficulties in mathematics which cannot be attributed to low intelligence, sensory deficits or economic deprivation.

Characteristics of Children with Learning Disabilities

Children with learning disabilities are a heterogeneous group. These children are a diverse group of individuals, exhibiting potential difficulties in many different areas. For example, one child with a learning disability may experience significant reading problems, while another may experience no reading problems whatsoever, but has significant difficulties with written expression.

Lerner (2000) identified nine learning and behavioural characteristics of individuals with learning disabilities:

- Disorders of attention
- Reading difficulties
- Poor motor abilities
- Written language difficulties
- Oral language difficulties
- Social skills deficits
- Psychological process deficits
- Quantitative disorders
- Information processing problems

Types of Learning Disability

Learning disabilities can be categorized either by the type of information processing that is affected or by the specific difficulties caused by a processing deficit.

Learning disabilities usually fall under these categories:

Classification of Learning Disabilities

Learning Disabilities can be classified as follows:

1. **Dyslexia:** It is a condition where child has difficulty in reading, writing, spelling, speaking etc.
2. **Dyscalculia:** The child has problem in doing maths problems, understanding time, using money.
3. **Dysgraphia:** In this Dysgraphia child will have problems with handwriting, spelling, organizing ideas etc.
4. **Dyspraxia (Sensory Integration Disorder):** The child has Problem with eye-hand coordination, balance, manual dexterity etc.
5. **Dysphasia/Aphasia:** In this condition the child has Problem with understanding spoken language, poor reading comprehension.
6. **Auditory Processing Disorder:** The child has difficulty with hearing differences between sounds and also problem with reading, comprehension, language.
7. **Visual Processing Disorder:** In this condition the child has difficulty in interpreting visual information, like maps, charts, symbols, pictures.

Identification of Learning Disabilities

Learning disabilities are often identified by school psychologists, clinical psychologists, and neuro psychologists through a combination of intelligence testing, academic achievement testing, classroom performance, and social interaction and aptitude. Other areas of assessment include perception, cognition, memory, attention, and language abilities. The resulting information is used to determine whether a child's academic performance is commensurate with his or her cognitive ability. If a child's cognitive ability is much higher than his or her academic performance, the student is often diagnosed with a learning disability. The DSM-IV and many school systems and government programs diagnose learning disabilities in this way (DSM-IV uses the term "disorder" rather than "disability".)

Although the discrepancy model has dominated the school system for many years, there has been substantial criticism of this approach among researchers. Recent research has provided little evidence that a discrepancy between formally measured IQ and achievement is a clear indicator of LD. Furthermore, diagnosing on the basis of a discrepancy does not predict the effectiveness of treatment. Low academic achievers who do not have a discrepancy with IQ (i.e. their IQ scores are also low) appear to benefit from treatment just as much as low academic achievers who do have a discrepancy with IQ (i.e. their IQ scores are higher than their academic performance).

Management

Special Education

Special education or special needs education is the education of students with special needs in a way that addresses the students' individual differences and needs. Ideally, this process involves the individually planned and systematically monitored arrangement of teaching procedures, adapted equipment and materials, accessible settings, and other interventions designed to help learners with special needs achieve a higher level of personal self-sufficiency and success in school and community than would be available if the student were only given access to a typical classroom education.

Another large issue is the lack of resources enabling individuals with special needs to receive an education in the developing world. As a consequence, 98 percent of children with special needs in developing countries do not have access to education.

Special Schools

A special school is a school catering for students who have special educational needs due to severe learning difficulties, physical disabilities or behavioural problems. Special schools may be specifically designed, staffed and resourced to provide the appropriate special education for children with additional needs.

Special schools provide individualized education, addressing specific needs. Student-teacher ratios are kept low, often 6:1 or lower depending upon the needs of the children. Special schools will also have other facilities for the development of children with special needs, such as soft play areas, sensory rooms, or swimming pools, which are vital for the therapy of certain conditions. Schools use different approaches to provide special education services to identified students. These can be broadly grouped into four categories, depending on the contact the student with special needs has with non-disabled students as follows:

- **Inclusion:** Is an approach in which, students with special educational needs spend all or at least more than half, of the school day with students who do not have special educational needs. Because inclusion can require substantial modification of the general curriculum, most schools use it only for selected students with mild to moderate special needs, for which is accepted as a best practice. Specialized services may be provided inside or outside the regular classroom, depending on the type of service. Students may occasionally leave the regular classroom to attend smaller, more intensive instructional sessions in a resource room, or to receive other related services that might require specialized equipment or might be disruptive to the rest of the class, such as speech and language therapy, occupational therapy, physical therapy, rehabilitation counseling or might require greater privacy, such as counseling sessions.

- **Mainstreaming** refers to the practice of educating students with special needs in classes with non-disabled students during specific time periods based on their skills. Students with special needs are segregated in separate classes exclusively for students with special needs for the rest of the school day.
- **Segregation** in a separate classroom or special school exclusively for students with special needs: In this model, students with special needs spend no time in classes with non-disabled students. Segregated students may attend the same school where regular classes are provided, but spend all instructional time exclusively in a separate classroom for students with special needs. If their special class is located in an ordinary school, they may be provided opportunities for social integration outside the classroom, e.g., by eating meals with non-disabled students. Alternatively these students may attend a special school.
- **Exclusion:** A student who does not receive instruction in any school is excluded from school. Historically, most students with special needs have been excluded from school. Such exclusion still affects about 23 million disabled children worldwide, particularly in poor, rural areas of developing countries. It may also occur when a student is in hospital, housebound or detained by the criminal justice system. These students may receive one-on-one instruction or group instruction. Students who have been suspended or expelled are not considered excluded in this sense.
- **Full Time special education:** A special school is a school catering for students who have special educational needs due to severe learning difficulties, physical disabilities or behavioural problems. Special schools may be specifically designed, staffed and resourced to provide the appropriate special education for children with additional needs.
- **Resource rooms or classrooms** (sometimes smaller classrooms) where a special education program can be delivered to a student with a disability. It is for the student who qualifies for either a special class or regular class placement but needs some special

instruction in an individualized or small group setting for a portion of the day. Individual needs are supported in resource rooms as defined by the student's IEP. Sometimes this form of support is called Resource and Withdrawal (or pulls out). The child getting this type of support will receive some time in the resource room which refers to the withdrawal portion of the day and sometime in the regular classroom with modifications and or accommodations which is the resource support in the regular classroom.

Teacher's Role in Resource Room

Teachers in the resource room have a challenging role as they need to design all instruction to meet the specific needs of the students they service to maximize their learning potential. The resource room teachers work closely with the child's regular classroom teacher and the parents to ensure support is indeed helping the student to reach their full potential. The teacher follows the IEP and will take part in the IEP review meetings. The teacher will also work very closely with other professionals and Para professionals to support the specific student. Usually the resource room teacher will work with small groups helping in one to one situations when possible.

Management of Learning Problems

The special education classroom may be the only place where children with LD will be equipped with stress management skills which will become increasingly more important as the pressures to achieve academically increase.

When a child is diagnosed with learning disabilities, all of the attention is focused on helping the child. However, parents also need assistance in coping with their own feelings and frustrations.

Research has shown that perceived far more stress in their role as parents than did parents of children without learning problems.

The management of the student with learning disability (LD) begins with quality instruction, even before the student is identified as having an LD. Inadequate exposure to quality instruction may account for the student's learning failure as early as kindergarten or first grade. It is generally believed that early intervention with quality instruction improves outcomes for all students with learning failure (including those with LD) and that it is more difficult to educate students with LD when they are older. Thus, quality instruction should be provided early and should be provided before attempts are made to identify learning disability among children. This approach is the rationale for the No Child Left Behind Act (NCLB), which requires schools to provide "highly qualified" teachers. Quality instruction is also required upon identification of LD.

Intervention

Some forms of learning disability are incurable. However, with appropriate cognitive/academic interventions, many can be overcome. Individuals with learning disabilities can face unique challenges that are often pervasive throughout the lifespan. Depending on the type and severity of the disability, interventions may be used to help the individual learn strategies that will foster future success. Some interventions can be quite simplistic, while others are intricate and complex. Teachers and parents will be a part of the intervention in terms of how they aid the individual in successfully completing different tasks. School psychologists quite often help to design the intervention, and coordinate the execution of the intervention with teachers and parents. Social support improves the learning for students with learning disabilities.

Role of Parents and Teachers in Management

Parents and teachers play an important role in management of problems related LD. Parenting children with learning disabilities presents special challenges, not only with the child's everyday problems, but also the associated social and emotional problems of school failure. Better coping strategies and parent groups can provide both skill training and emotional support for parents of children with learning disabilities.

Teaching children that many people have overcome difficulties to become successful is another valuable parenting strategy. One way to do this is to read or play tapes of biographies in which children or adults have had to struggle to achieve their goals-adventures where the characters got lost or had to fight sharks or other beasts; stories of achieving despite illness or disability; or stories of fighting prejudice or unfairness. Children enjoy and benefit from discussing these kinds of challenges.

The teacher plays many roles in the classroom. An important role is the recognition of pupils with learning difficulties. The teacher must be able to appraise the situation and decide on a course of action. One course of action may result in identifying a child with a possible learning disability. Understanding the process and protocol of identifying a learning disabled child may help the teacher in understanding this important role.

Teachers and others concerned about students with learning disabilities can develop an understanding of learning disabilities as a field of study. Although they may not be readily recognized in the early years, learning disabilities extend across the life span. They are closely associated with bio neurological differences among people, and they may manifest themselves in one or more areas of human endeavor, including cognition, attention, social behaviour and related social factors such as self-concept, language, and especially academic learning. As the field has matured, researchers have built a strong body of evidence showing that effective methods can address these problems. Teachers can help individuals with learning disabilities achieve at levels that allow them to live satisfying and fulfilling lives.

Parents, teachers, and other professionals discover a child's learning disability early and provide the right kind of help. It can give the child a chance to develop skills needed to lead a success full and productive life. A study by National Institutes of Health showed that 67 percent of young students who were at risk for reading difficulties became average or above average readers after receiving help in the early grades (2006).

Parents and teachers also boost children's self-esteem by seeking out what they can do well and fostering and supporting these areas to the build. Whether it is an art form, science, nature, photography, computer work, selling things, inventing, or telling stories, children with learning disabilities need parental support to become the best in this area at home and to bring their talent into school. It won't help them feel better about their academic performance, but it will help them feel better about themselves.

Parents and teachers of children with learning disabilities can help them by providing clear structuring of time and space. To help children with structuring space, visual aids can be useful. For example, shelves can be used instead of drawers so children can see where things belong and how to put them back. The use of other visual cues, such as lists or labels, can augment efforts to help children organize tasks and belongings.

A large number of children with learning disabilities have language learning disabilities, which means they have trouble in language, listening, and following instructions. Because of this, it is also helpful if parents and teachers limit the number of words used in giving directions, using simple phrases such as, *'Go upstairs','Close the window', 'Come down' etc.*

Coping Up of Problems

Learning disabilities may also be mild, moderate, or severe. Students differ too, in their coping skills. According to Bowe (2005), "some learn to adjust to LD so well that they 'pass' as not having a disability, while others struggle throughout their lives to even do 'simple' things. Despite these differences, LD always begins in childhood and always is a life-long condition".

In India around 13-14 per cent of all school children suffer from learning disorders. Unfortunately most teachers fail to lend a sympathetic ear to the problems of children. As a result these children are branded as failures. Despite the fact that, the learning disabilities which includes a group of disorders like listening, speaking, reading, writing and mathematics etc is a known class room disorders, it has not reached its optimum awareness levels in the schools in our country.

Neuropsychological differences can impact the accurate perception of social cues with peers. A diagnosis of a learning disability can be potentially devastating to an individual and their family. Both the individual and their family need to learn methods of coping with the effects of the disorder; they also need to learn how to cope with the disorder emotionally. Stress related to the disorder can accumulate, making the coping process difficult. Stigmas that friends/family/peers have about the learning disorder can also contribute to the stress level the individual feels. Learning disabilities are often present throughout the lifespan, so learning appropriate and effective methods of coping are essential to successful management of the disorder.

Present Study

The major aim of the study was to understand the adjustment problems of children with learning disability in comparison with normal achievers based on the perception of parents and teachers. The scope of the study also includes the study of relationship between special education and adjustment problems and also coping up of problems by children with learning disability.

In India, it is estimated that approximately Specific Learning Disability (SPLD) affects almost 5-15 per cent of school going children but there is a lack of awareness about specific learning disability among the teachers, parent's community and general public. The LD movement in India is of a recent origin and is today comparable with that of its western counterpart.

Teachers play an important role in any educational system.Teacher is an artist who moulds and shapes the physical, intellectual and moral powers of children. In any normal school one can find children with mild learning disabilities. If the learning disabilities are unnoticed, unanswered, ignored and such children's needs are not met in regular class rooms or special education within the school; the aim of universalisation of elementary education and equalization of educational opportunity cannot be fulfilled. It brings scholastic backwardness in these children. Teachers generally did not understand and accept the child's limitations. Teachers either ignore the deficiency or blame it on the children's personality branding it as laziness, neglect attitude or aggression. The child, who is unable to handle the academic pressure, faces adjustment problems. Hence, a need was felt to identify and to study the adjustment problems of children with learning disability and the possible determinants of the problems.

A comparative study of adjustment problems of normal achievers that is children without learning disability helps to understand whether the problems faced by children are common during elementary school age or whether these exists any difference between children with LD and without LD.

Generally LD is identified during elementary school age. Kavita *et al.*, (2012), also mentioned that second and third grade is most suitable to intervene through proper remedial strategies for children with LD. Hence, it was planned to study the problems of children who were studying 3rd, 4th and 5th grades.

Parents and teachers of elementary school children have many reactions towards children's, adjustment in areas like academic, home, emotional, social etc., when the child has to master skill in these areas. Parents feel happy if the child is successful in making adjustments and they may be worried, experience stress and feel bad if their child could not compete with their peer groups.

Many parents experienced lack of support from their family members, friends, neighbors and school personnel. Most of the parents had worries about their child's future, felt more guilt and embarrassment within the family, neighbors and school due to name callings and fights. Hence, assessment of parental perception of emotional reaction towards their children adjustments has been selected as one of the variables.

The existence of special education schools for children with LD are very rare. Recently with the initiation by the Government, resource rooms are introduced in the Government schools. However, the teachers have not received necessary training to identify and guide children with LD. Hence, it was planned to assess how far special education schools help to manage the problems related to LD.

Presence of LD causes stress to parents and students. Both the individual and their family need to learn methods of coping with the effects of the disorder. Child also needs to learn how to cope with the disorder emotionally. Individualized remedial education will be helpful for children to cope up with the problems successfully.Therefore, the impact of SE on coping up of problems by children was also included as one of the variables to understand the role of SE in management of problems related to LD.

With these back ground the present study was designed with the following objectives.

Objectives

1. To identify the sample children with learning disability using Identification of Learning Disability Inventory (LDDI) (Hammill and Bryant, 1998).
2. To compare IQ, behaviour problems and parental perception of emotional reaction towards children's adjustments of children with and without learning disability.
3. To assess the relationship among demographic variables and teachers' perception of behaviour problems among children.

4. To assess the relationship among demographic variables and parents' perception of emotional reactions towards children's adjustments.
5. To assess the relationship among LD variables, behaviour problems and parental perception of emotional reactions towards children's adjustment.
6. To assess the relationship among SE variables, behaviour problems, parental perception of emotional reactions towards children's adjustment and coping up of problems by children.
7. To find out the determinants of outcome variables.

Next chapter deals with the review of literature.

2

Review of Literature

Research related to the problem of learning disability has been conducted in USA since 1980s. But the focus on this problem has been highlighted in Indian origin for the past decade onwards.

Several reported studies have focused on academic competency, social acceptance, behaviour problems, adjustments of learning disability children and majority of the studies were comparative studies with non learning disabled children.

The task of presenting a review of relevant reported studies is rather difficult as the studies were conducted in different contexts. However, an attempt is made to sift some relevant reported studies having some bearing on the main purpose of the study. To improve the clarity, the available related literature in the area of adjustments and learning disability were grouped under different heads as follows:

- Adjustment Problems among Children with and without LD
- Behaviour Problems among Children with and without LD
- Relationship of Demographic Variables and LD
- Children with Learning Disability
  - Prevalence of Learning Disability
  - Problems Related to Learning Disability
  - Perception of Parents, Children and Teachers about Learning Disability
- Management of Problems Related to Learning Disability
  - Children with Special Education
  - Coping up of problems related to Learning Disability

Adjustment Problems among Children with and without LD

Adjustment is a process by which a living organism maintains a balance between the needs and the circumstances.

The term adjustment is often used as a synonym for accommodation and adaptation. According to Monroe, (1990), adjustment is used to emphasize the individual's struggle to survive in his or her social and physical environment.

An effort was made to present studies related to adjustments of children in different areas viz., social, emotional, academic and also adjustments in general. Studies conducted in India and at abroad are separated depending on the availability, to improve clarity in presentation.

General Adjustment Problems

Indian Studies

Raju and Rahamtulla (2000), examined the adjustment problems of school students from urban and rural schools of Visakhapatnam district. The variables included for the study apart from adjustments (family, social, academic, financial and emotional) are age, gender, class, type of school etc. The study was conducted on a sample of 461 students (197 boys, 264 girls) randomly selected from the various government and private schools from urban and rural areas of Visakhapatnam district, Andhra Pradesh. A standardized questionnaire developed by Jain (1972) was adopted for the study. The data was analyzed to examine the influence of individual factors on adjustment variables. The major findings of the study have shown that adjustment of school children is primarily dependent on the school variables like the class in which they are studying, the medium of instruction present in the school, and the type of management of the school. Parental education and occupation of the school children also significantly influenced adjustment.

In yet another Indian study, Sunita and Manju (2015), examined adjustment problems of LD children and the role of parental involvement in adjustment of elementary school children with learning disabilities. The study was conducted on a sample of 89 students (59 boys, 30 girls) randomly selected from the various government and private schools of chandighar. A standardized scale on parental involvement developed by Chopra and Sahoo (2006) was used for the study. The major findings of the study have shown that 'adjustments of elementary school children with learning disability is significantly correlated with parental home involvement. Home involvement significantly affected the adjustments of the school children. No significant correlations were found between adjustments and parents' school involvement and parental involvement through parent teacher associations.

Abroad Studies

In a study comparing children with LD and without LD Michal Al-Yagon along with Mario (2004), examined patterns of close relationships among school-age children with learning disabilities (LD) as manifested in their attachment style, their self-perceived loneliness, their sense of coherence, and teacher ratings of their academic functioning. The study also aimed to further explore predictors of positive adjustment for children with LD. The sample comprised 98 children with LD from regular classes in four Israeli public elementary schools, and 98 non-LD children from the same classes. Significant group differences emerged in attachment styles and adjustment. Attachment style significantly correlated with socio-emotional adjustment but not with academic functioning.

The following studies focused on social adjustment of children.

Social Adjustment

Bryan (1974), experimented to determine the peer popularity of children classified as learning disabled. The method employed was to administer a socio- metric technique to 62 third, fourth, and fifth grade children in which there was at least one learning disabled child. An analysis of variance was computed for votes received on scales of social attraction and social rejection by learning disabled and comparison children matched on variables of sex, race, and classroom. The results indicated that learning disabled children, particularly white male and female, were significantly less attractive and more rejected than comparison children.

Paul (1990), in a study compared 86 children with learning disabilities (LD) with 86 matched children without learning disabilities (NLD) on three domains of variables: social problem-solving skill, teacher-rated school behaviour and competence, and family background. The children with LD and the NLD group differed on variables in all three domains. More specifically, the children with LD were able to generate fewer alternatives for solving social problem situations, showed less tolerance for frustration and less adaptive assertiveness, and had more overall classroom behaviour problems and less personal and social competence in a variety of areas as rated by teachers. Children having LD also showed more family background difficulties (e.g., lack of educational stimulation at home, economic difficulties).

Juvonen and George (1992), examined the social adjustment of 46 children with learning disabilities (LDs) and 199 children without LDs who were integrated full-time in 3rd-grade. No differences were found in the proportions of children with LDs and without LDs across accepted and unpopular socio-metric groups. Two thirds of children with LDs had at least 1 reciprocal friend, and more than half had a friendship with a classmate without LDs. Girls with LDs received the highest number of negative nominations and were the least preferred. Group comparisons of socially adjusted and non-adjusted children, with and without LDs, showed that teachers perceived the socially adjusted children with LDs to be less socially and academically competent than adjusted children with LDs.

Sater and French (1998), investigated the social competencies of learning disabled (LD) and non-LD low achieving (LA) children in two studies. First, the social status of 101 LD, 156 LA, and 608 normally achieving children were assessed using peer socio-metric ratings. LD and LA children received statistically significant lower ratings than normally achieving students. LD children were lower in social status than non-LD children, but did not differ significantly from LA children. Furthermore, approximately 70% of the LD children did not experience social rejection. In Study 2, parent and teacher behaviour ratings were obtained for rejected and accepted LD and LA children to assess the comparability of these populations. Both LD and LA rejected children exhibited lower social competence and a greater incidence of behaviour problems than did accepted children. Contrary to predictions, no differences between LD boys and girls were found in either study.

Shirley and Milich (1999), examined the response of boys and girls with or without learning disabilities to social failure. Children participated in two dyadic interactions with experimental confederates: an unfriendly interaction and a friendly one. The children's behaviour was videotaped, and they answered questions following each interaction. The children with learning disabilities were found to be hyper responsive to both interactions: They felt significantly worse following the unfriendly one and significantly better following the friendly interaction.

After three decades, Bryan (2000), reviewed a series of studies which investigated the socio-metric status, social behaviour, and social relationship of learning disabled children in classroom observations and laboratory studies. The results indicated that a significant number of learning disabled children are experiencing difficulty in eliciting positive responses from others and in establishing friendships with peers.

Yet another study was conducted on social acceptance and learning disability by Andreassi and Cristia (2007), who examined the relationships among social cognition, externalizing behaviour, and social acceptance in children with and without learning disabilities. It was hypothesized that social-cognitive accuracy and externalizing behaviour would mediate differences observed in social acceptance between children with and without learning disabilities. School-identified children with learning disabilities (N = 55) in grades 3, 4, 5 were compared to their non-identified peers (N= 631) in terms of social acceptance. Social acceptance was determined using peer nominations of liked most and liked least, which were converted into an overall social preference score for each child. When it was determined that children's learning disability status accounted for a small but significant portion of the variance in children's social acceptance (1.3%). Mediation tests were conducted to determine if externalizing behaviour or social cognitive accuracy functioned as mediators in the observed relationship. Externalizing behaviour was assessed through teacher report on the Child Behaviour Checklist. Social-cognitive accuracy was determined by calculating the extent to which individual children's reports of peer groups in their classrooms matched the social groups derived through Social Cognitive Mapping. The results indicated that externalizing behaviour partially mediated the relationship between learning disabilities and social acceptance. No evidence was found that social-cognitive accuracy functioned as a mediator.

The following studies are related emotional and school adjustments of children with LD and Non LD.

Emotional Adjustment

Indian Study

In an Indian study, Gitanjali (2004), studied on personality characteristics of primary school students with learning disabilities and their non learning disabled peers. Personality characteristics of 108 boys and girls of ages, 8, 9 and 10 years with learning disabilities in 3rd, 4th and 5th grades in rural and urban primary schools of Andhra Pradesh, India. The subjects were identified based on their scholastic achievement on a spelling dictation test, an oral reading test, a reading comprehension test and an arithmetic test developed specifically for the purpose, along with mental ability test, Raven's Standard Progressive Matrices and Draw a man test, an adapted version of the Children's Personality Questionnaire (CPQ) was administrated to the subjects with learning disabilities. Examination of scores obtained by LD and NLD subjects on CPQ portrays the LD child as having problems in social and emotional adjustment. Further, the older LD children tended to show a more maladaptive behavioural disposition than the younger, and there was a significant gender effects among LD children.

Abroad Studies

Mario and Michal Al-Yagon (2004), in another study reported on the role of attachment-based factors (children's attachment style, children's appraisal of teacher as a secure base, and teacher's feelings of closeness to child) in explaining differences in Israeli children's socio emotional adjustment (self-rated sense of coherence, loneliness) and academic functioning (teacher-rated). The sample comprised 98 children with learning disorders from general education classes in four public elementary schools and 107 typically developing children from the same classes. Significant intergroup differences emerged in socio emotional and academic adjustment as well as attachment-based factors. Moreover, attachment-based factors were significantly correlated with adjustment measures and significantly mediated the association between learning disorders and socio emotional adjustment.

Margaret and Margaret (2010), compared emotional and academic adjustment among LD children. They investigated about early adolescents (Grades 6-8) with multiple learning disabilities (LD; reading and math) in inclusive settings to adolescents with single LD (reading or math) and typically achieving (TA) peers regarding their psychosocial functioning in two areas of adolescent well-being: emotional adjustment and school functioning. The *Behaviour Assessment System for Children* (Reynolds & Kamphaus, 1998) Self-Report of Personality for adolescents was used to determine well-being. One hundred twenty middle school students (15 boys and 15 girls in each group) were the sample of the study. The results confirmed that adolescents with multiple LD (reading and math) reported poorer functioning (i.e., higher *T* scores) on school maladjustment, clinical maladjustment, emotional symptoms index, attitude to school, a typicality, and depression when compared to TA peers but not when compared to peers with a single LD (reading or math). All three groups differed from the TA group (but not from each other) on sense of inadequacy, with the multiple LD group reporting the highest *T* scores. Additional analyses indicated significant differences between girls and boys, regardless of disability status. Girls reported higher *T* scores on the emotional symptoms index, social stress, and depression, but boys reported greater school maladjustment and sensation seeking.

The following studies are related academic adjustment of children with and without learning disabilities

Academic Adjustment

During elementary school years children start learning academic skills like reading, writing and arithmetic's. Problems with visual and auditory processing, memory and attention are associated with academic adjustments of children.

Chapman (1988), investigated about academic self-concept, academic locus of control, and achievement expectations over a 2-year period for 78 children identified as learning disabled (LD) and 71 non learning disabled, normally achieving children (NLD). The LD children had no remedial program for their learning problems and had not been classified by the schools as LD. The data were collected while the sample was in junior high school. Five schools participated in the project. The results indicated that in comparison with NLD students, the LD children had lower self-perceptions of ability, showed signs of learned helplessness, and reported lower achievement expectations. These differences were well established at the start of Year 1 of the project and remained consistent through to the end of Year 2. The hypothesis that LD children not receiving remedial help would develop increasingly negative affective characteristics was not supported. Correlation and regression data showed that academic self-concept scores were the single best predictor of achievement levels. The author opined that negative school-related attitudes develop early in the school lives of LD children and remain negative but consistent through high school.

James (2002), reported on the behavioural characteristics of children with learning disabilities (LD) compared to average achievers. Longitudinal studies over a 3-year period beginning in the first and second grades showed that children with LD, as a heterogeneous group, displayed a persistent pattern of maladaptive classroom behaviour that distinguished them from average achieving peers and that was associated with continued underachievement over time. Subsequently, children with LD in the longitudinal sample were clustered into seven different subtypes that represented attention problems, conduct and classroom management problems, withdrawn-dependent behaviour, and normal behaviour. Although no differences in achievement were found initially between behavioural subtypes, children in the attention and conduct problem subtypes had poorer academic outcomes 3 years later, compared to those in the withdrawn subtype and those who had no significant behaviour problems.

Hornstra and Denessen (2010), examined teacher attitudes toward dyslexia and the effects of these attitudes on teacher expectations and the academic achievement of students with dyslexia compared to students without learning disabilities. The attitudes of 30 regular education teachers toward dyslexia were determined using both an implicit measure and an explicit, self-report measure. Achievement scores for 307 students were also obtained. Implicit teacher attitudes toward dyslexia related to teacher ratings of student achievement on a writing task and also to student achievement on standardized tests of spelling but not math for those students with dyslexia. Self-reported attitudes of the teachers toward dyslexia did not relate to any of the outcome measures. Neither the implicit nor the explicit measures of teacher attitudes related to teacher expectations.

No Indian studies were reported in the area of academic adjustment of LD and NLD children.

From the above mentioned studies on adjustment problems of children in general and those in comparison with LD children in different adjustments like social, emotional and academic areas compared to NLD children, the following findings can be noted.

- Adjustment of school children is primarily dependent on the school variables like the class in which they are studying, the medium of instruction present in the school, and the type of management of the school. Parental education and occupation of the school children also significantly influenced adjustment.
- Learning disabled children, particularly white male and female, were significantly less attractive and more rejected than comparison children (Bryan 1974).
- Children having LD showed more family background difficulties (like lack of educational stimulation at home, economic difficulties etc.
- Teachers perceived the socially adjusted children with LDs to be less socially and academically competent than adjusted children with LDs.
- Both LD and Low achievers rejected children exhibited lower social competence and a greater incidence of behaviour problems than did accepted children. No differences between LD boys and girls were found.
- Significant differences were found between girls and boys, regardless of disability status. Reported that girls had higher *T* scores on the emotional symptoms index, social stress, and depression, but boys reported greater school maladjustment and sensation seeking.
- The LD child had problems in social and emotional adjustment. The older LD children tended to show a more maladaptive behavioural disposition than the younger, and there was a significant gender effects among LD children.
- Children with LD, as a heterogeneous group, displayed a persistent pattern of maladaptive classroom behaviour that distinguished them from average achieving peers and that was associated with continued underachievement over time.
- Negative school-related attitudes develop early in the school lives of LD children and remain negative but consistent through high school (Chapman 1988).

Behaviour Problems among Children with and without LD

The following studies discuss about behaviour problems of children with and without learning disabilities.

Abroad Studies

In one early study Stephanie and David (1986), investigated parents reports on social competence and behavioural problems of 123 learning disabled boys aged 6-11 who referred for a psycho educational assessment at the center of disorders of communication at the University of Vermont . One parent of each boy completed the Child Behaviour Check List developed by Achenbach and Edelblock (1983). On average the parents of LD boys reported significantly lower levels of social competence and more behaviour problems than normative samples of parents. On the social competence scales, the LD boys were significantly lower than the normative samples in their participation in activities, their social involvement and school performance. On the behaviour problem scales, the LD boys had significantly higher scores for both externalizing and "internalizing" types of problems, including problems related to depression, uncommunicativeness, obsessive-compulsive behaviours, social withdrawal, hyperactivity, aggressiveness and "delinquency" to a compared sample of other clinically referred boys, a significantly larger proportion of LD boys showed a higher active profile pattern and smaller proportions showed profile patterns indicated of depressed, social withdrawal aggressive behaviour and delinquency. There were significant but low positive correlation between IQ scores on the Wechsler's intelligence scale for children-revised and social competence scores and negative correlation between IQ scores and behaviour problem scores.

Symons and Greene (1996), assessed behaviour problems among students, using multiple reporters of problem behaviour to predict clinical referral of adolescents with Learning Disabilities. Ratings of behavioural and emotional problems at the start of a school year were used to predict referral for mental health assistance. Participants were 11 to 16-year-old adolescents with learning disabilities who attended a residential school. Reports of problem behaviour consisted of internalizing and externalizing behaviour on the parent and teacher reports of the Child Behaviour Checklist, ADHD behaviours on the home and school forms of the Children's Attention and Adjustment Survey, and depressive symptoms on the Children's Depression Inventory (CDI). Students referred for mental health services had higher scores than adolescents not referred on teacher ratings of externalizing behaviour, inattention, and conduct problems, as well as self-reports of depressive symptomatology, and were more likely to have scored above clinical cutoff scores on the first two measures as well as on parent reports of internalizing behaviours. There were correlations in the various kinds of problem behaviour rated by teachers, parent ratings were also inter-correlated, and CDI ratings correlated with both teacher and parent ratings of internalizing behaviour. The sample were adolescents.

Susan (1998), documented on similarities and differences in the domain-specific and global self-evaluations of 235 normally achieving, 118 learning-disabled, and 70 behaviourally disordered adolescents. Factor analysis revealed eight discrete self-concept domains for each group. The importance of success in each domain was similar for each group, as were processes predicting level of self-worth. Students with high self-worth evaluated themselves positively in domains of importance, whereas students with low self-worth reported much less favorable self-evaluations. Moreover, those with high self worth were better able to discount areas of weakness than were those with low self-worth. Correlations between specific domains deemed important and self-worth were also very similar across groups. Differences among groups involved the level of scores in that learning-disabled and behaviourally disordered students reported lower cognitive competence and peer likability than did normally achieving students. Behaviourally disordered students also reported more negative perceptions of their conduct. Both special education groups evidenced more negative self-worth with greater discrepancies between importance and negative self-evaluations, particularly in domains salient to the difficulties related to their educational status. However, the sample were adolescents.

Lardieri, Blaches and Swanson (2000), investigated whether (a) siblings of children with and without learning disabilities differed in terms of psychological adjustment and perceived impact of their target brother or sister; and (b) whether parents of learning disability and without learning disability children differed in terms of perceived stress and burden. Based on child behaviour check list scores of target child behaviour, families were divided into four groups: (a) No LD and no behaviour problems, (b) Ld only (c) Behaviour problems only and (d) LD and BP; Siblings and their parents were interviewed in their homes. Regardless of whether the target child was learning disabled or without learning disabled, parent reports CBPL differentially reflected the presence of behaviour problems. The results indicated that (a) LD and NLD siblings differed in their perception of quality of their sibling's relationships and self-repots of their own behaviour, and (b) the parents of children reported to have behaviour problems with and without LD reported high levels of perceived burden.

James (2002), compared the behavioural characteristics of children with learning disabilities (LD) with average achievers. Longitudinal studies over a 3-years period beginning in the first and second grades showed that children with LD, as a heterogeneous group, displayed a persistent pattern of maladaptive classroom behaviour that distinguished them from average achieving peers and that was associated with continued underachievement over time. Subsequently, children with LD in the longitudinal sample were clustered into seven different subtypes that represented attention problems, conduct and classroom management problems, withdrawn-dependent behaviour, and normal behaviour.

In another study Michaels (2004), examined parent reports of behavioural and family functioning for 59 boys with learning disabilities (LD) and 65 non disabled boys (NLD) of ages 6 to 12 years. Parents completed the Child Behaviour Checklist (CBCL) and the Family Adaptability and Cohesion Evaluation Scale (FACES III). Boys with LD were reported as having significantly more behaviour problems of both the Internalizing and Externalizing types than NLD boys. Individual scales yielded group differences indicating higher scores (more problems) for the group with LD on the Hyperactive, Schizoid or Anxious, Depressed, and Obsessive Compulsive Scales, but no differences on the Aggressive or Social Withdrawal scales. Furthermore, families of boys with LD tended to score more frequently in the extreme (disturbed) range of family functioning. However, boys of families in the extreme range did not have more behaviour problems than the boys of other families.

Ron and Nancy (2007), conducted a comparative analysis of the effects of direct instruction, cooperative learning, and independent learning instructional practices on the classroom behaviour of students with behaviour disorders. Results indicated that there were distinct differences in the classroom behaviour of the students during the direct instruction condition. In this condition, they displayed higher rates of on-task behaviour and lower rates of disruptive behaviour relative to the cooperative learning and independent learning conditions. There appeared to be little or no differences between the classroom behaviour of the students during the cooperative learning condition and that during the independent learning condition. The results suggested (a) that the instructional sequence underlying direct instruction practices reduces the disruptive behaviour of students, and (b) that instructional practices may serve as an aversive stimuli in classrooms.

The over view of above studies showed that:

- There were significant but low positive correlation between IQ scores on the Wechsler intelligence scale for children and social competence scores and negative correlation between IQ scores and behaviour problem scores
- There were correlations in the various kinds of problem behaviour rated by teachers, parent ratings were also inter correlated, and CDI ratings correlated with both teacher and parent ratings of internalizing behaviour.
- The parents of LD and NLD children reported to have behaviour problems with and without LD reported high levels of perceived burden.
- Boys with LD were reported as having significantly more behaviour problems of both the internalizing and externalizing types than NLD boys.

Relationship of Demographic Variables and LD

Demographic variables included in the present study were child, parent and family. Studies conducted on relation of demographic variables with LD and NLD children are presented under these headings.

Child Variables

Abroad Studies

Konstantareas and Homatidis (1989), studied the Parental perception of learning-disabled children's adjustment problems and related stress. Mothers and fathers of learning-disabled (LD) children rated their children's problems on the Child Behaviour Checklist (CBCL) and the stress they experienced as a result of each problem. Data were examined as a function of (a) the child's sex, age, birth order, IQ, discrepancy IQ, and degree of LD; (b) the parents' age, locus of control, and self-concept; and (c) family SES, family size, and mother's working status. Both parents rated externalizing behaviours higher than internalizing. Boys were rated as significantly more problematic and stressful than girls. Greater child adjustment problems and concomitant parental stress were reported by the younger half of the maternal sample and their spouses, and by fathers with a lower self-concept and their wives. Although mothers did not differ from fathers in behaviour ratings, they reported greater stress in response to them. This was particularly true of mothers of middle or upper SES with an external locus of control.

Girls with LD may be underestimated, putting them at risk for academic, social and emotional challenges. Teachers refer boys more often than girls for assistance prior to special educators. In one review Green *et al.* (1996) reported some factors that lead to significantly high reference of boys. Boys tend to have more externalizing problems. More optimistic views about girls were observed such as girls will improve as they mature. Social expectations for girl's academic learning were not consistently high. Girls exhibit more passive behaviours such as sitting and daydreaming. So they are less likely to be identified than boys (Shaywitz *et al.* 1990). Eme (1992) reported the gender ratio in LD as 3.5 to 5 males for one female. Smith, (2004) revealed that boys are 1.5 times more likely to be identified than girls are. Boys are far more likely to be identified as LD despite the research suggesting an equal incidence of LD among girls and boys. These could be linked to possible medical, maturational, sociological and brain organization factors.

Miglani *et al.*, (2011), conducted a study on the intelligence and achievement motivation among learning disabled children and non-learning disabled children. RSPM (Raven's Successive Progressive Matrices) was used to measure intelligence and GLAD (Grade Level Assessment Device, 1997) was used to measure need for motivation. No significant difference was observed in intelligence, but children without learning disabilities showed higher need for motivation than children with learning disabilities.

Indian Study

Patnaik (2011), studied the simultaneous and successive cognitive processes in normal and learning disabled children. She took ninety normal children from grades 3, 5 and 7 and sixty learning disabled children and graded them on the basis of their score on the RCPM (Raven's Colored Progressive Matrices) and Oriya Reading Comprehension Tests. It was observed that performance of both types of children (i.e. with and without disabilities) improved as a function of grade.

- Boys were rated as significantly more problematic and stressful than girls (Konstantareas and Homatidis, 1989)
- Gender ratio in LD was found to be 3.5 to 5 males for one female, boys are 1.5 or 6 times more likely to be identified than girls. Boys are far more likely to be identified as LD despite the research suggesting an equal incidence of LD among girls and boys (Smith, 2004).
- No significant difference was observed in intelligence, but children without learning disabilities showed higher need for motivation than children with learning disabilities.
- Performance of both types of children i.e. with and without disabilities improved as a function of grade (Patnaik, 2011).

Family and Parent Variables

Abroad Studies

Long back Wilson (1975) discovered that parental indulgence and infrequent punishment were associated with academic difficulties.

Rezique (1983) found that mother's educational level influenced children's academic achievement. Parents with poor educational levels may lack motivation and academic ambition, be unable to help in their children's schoolwork and may have a low index of suspicion of their learning disabilities, delaying diagnosis and remedial teaching.

Turnbull and Rueif (1997) interviewed 127 families of children with learning disabilities along with behavioural problems. The results revealed that families of LD children described home routines as challenging and disruptive due to the problem behaviour. Majority of the parents reported lack of close connection between disabled child and his/her sibling, find difficult time in establishing comfortable and connected relationships with the disabled child. Over half of the families indicated that it was impossible for them to participate in their preferred religious activities as a family unit. The parents did not give priority to community inclusion because of time and energy limitations, unavailability of other companion-ship and the family's and other's perceptions of worry, fear and embarrassment. Thus, families reported a tenuous inclusive life style.

Dyson (2006), investigated thirty pairs of fathers and mothers who had school-age children with mental retardation and other disabilities were compared with each other and with 32 father and mother pairs of parents of children without disabilities. Responses to family scales indicated that fathers and mothers of children with developmental disabilities did not differ from each other or from fathers and mothers of children without disabilities in parental stress, family social support, or family functioning. However, parents of children with disabilities experienced a disproportionately greater level of stress relating to their children than did those of children without disabilities. Fathers' and mothers' stress was associated with aspects of family functioning as perceived by themselves and their spouses.

Kausar and Munir (2008), investigated the social and emotional adjustment of adolescents living with single parents and those living with both parents. A sample of 90 adolescents was taken from schools of Rawalpindi (Pakistan). It was found that adolescents living with single parents were significantly less socio-emotionally adjusted than their counterparts from intact families. Findings highlighted the significance of family structure in particular, presence of parents for healthy psycho-social development of adolescents. However, the samples were adolescents.

From the above mentioned studies it can be interpreted that:

- That families of LD children described home routines as challenging and disruptive due to the problem behaviour.
- Parents of children with disabilities experienced a disproportionately greater level of stress relating to their children than did those of children without disabilities.
- Adolescents living with single parents were significantly less socio-emotionally adjusted than their counterparts from intact families.

Children with Learning Disability

Prevalence of Learning Disability

The following studies related to learning disability prevalence and diagnosis.

Indian Studies

In an Indian study, Vijayalakshmi *et al.*,(2011), conducted a cross sectional multi staged stratified randomized cluster sampling study to measure the prevalence of specific learning disability such as dyslexia, dysgraphia and dyscalculia among primary school children in a south Indian city. It was conducted among children aged 8-11 years from third and fourth standards. A six level screening approach that commenced with identification of scholastic backwardness followed by stepwise exclusion of impaired vision and hearing, chronic medical conditions and subnormal intelligence was carried out among these children. In the final step, the remaining children were subjected to specific tests for reading, comprehension, writing and mathematics. The prevalence of specific learning disabilities was 15.17 per cent in sampled children. Among these 12.5 per cent, 11.2 per cent and 10.5 per cent had dysgraphia, dyslexia and dyscalculia respectively. The study suggested that the prevalence of specific learning disability is at the higher side of previous estimations in India.

Kavita, Devi and Narang (2012), conducted a study to screen the poor performers of second and third grade for specific learning disabilities. A total of [illegible] children studying in public schools in Jhunjhunu district of Rajasthan were screened, out of which 30 specific learning disabled children having average or above average intelligence were assessed. Behavioural Checklist for Screening the Learning Disabled by Swarup and Mehta (2011) was used to find out specific learning disabilities in children. Quantitative and Qualitative analysis of scores evaluated that most of children have difficulties in visual processing, auditory processing, motor co-ordination and memory. Results further revealed that majority of children were deficit in language, cognitive and affective domains which are very crucial to the child's learning ability and performance.

Akhil and Tushar (2013), focused on prevalence and pattern of learning disability in school children. The sample of the study consisted of primary school children studying in English and Hindi medium schools of rural areas of Jaipur. The data was elicited through school teachers and students. Total population studied were 1156 (boys 668 and girls 488), age group was 6-13 years. Out of 148 positive cases (12.8 per cent), Dyslexia was seen in 32 (21.62 per cent) students. Dysgraphia was seen in 33 (22.30 per cent) students, Dyscalculia was seen in 23 (15.54 per cent) students. Mixed learning disorders was seen in 60 (40.50 per cent) students. The number of students having learning disability was higher age group. It was also noticed that with increase in number of siblings then, there is a decrease in number of positive cases. When gender is considered there is no difference in prevalence of learning disorders. It is more common in students from nuclear family. When the language of instruction is Hindi there are more chances of suffering from learning disability. There is more chances of person having learning disorder if he/she is right handed more large scale studies warranted to know the exact prevalence and patterns of learning disability in school going children.

Kamala (2014), while reviewing issues and challenges of Persons with Specific Learning Disability (SPLD) viewed that Specific Learning Disability is not visible as other disabilities such as visually impaired, hearing impaired and mentally challenged. In the developed countries like United States of America and Britain, already they have included specific learning disability category in the disability law. As in the case of India, Persons with Disability Act (PWD) is considered as one of the corner stone in the disability act but the specific learning disability category is not included in the Act. She reported that so far the rights of the specific learning disability students are hidden and forgotten by the Indian government like their disability. The teachers, parents' community and the students should be properly educated about the rights of the learning disability students.

Abroad Study

In an international study Grace and Janet (2012) compared the educational policies related to LD in India and Australia. The study sample were five English-medium independent primary schools in Bangalore and five independent primary schools in Adelaide of Australia. Findings showed that in the Indian schools, segregation was the norm. Funding for students with disabilities was charity-based and the recognition of learning support was minimal. In the Australian schools, inclusion was the norm. The demand for services was high and efforts at accommodation were constrained by funding criteria. In both contexts, definition of need and the quality of teaching were significant issues.

The overview of the above studies:

- The prevalence of specific leaning disability is at higher side of previous estimation in India.
- It was also noticed that with increase in number of siblings then, there is a decrease in number of positive cases.
- When gender is considered there is no difference in prevalence of learning disorders. It is more common in students from nuclear family.
- In majority of cases mixed learning disability was reported.

Problems Related to Learning Disability

General learning disability must be differentiated from specific learning difficulty (dyslexia) which means that the person has one difficulty such as in reading, writing or understanding, but has no problem with learning in other areas.

The following studies related to problems of children with and without learning disabilities, with regard to specific learning difficulty.

Abroad Studies

(a) Reading Problems

Daniels (1996), studied the co-existence of artistic talent and dyslexia. She made a case study of two world renowned artists, Chuck Close and Pat Buckley Moss, who were both dyslexic. She tried to find whether visual abilities needed to read were different from those needed for creative works of art or whether it was a verbal problem. Results showed that artistic talent can co-exist with dyslexia. Dyslexia either involves different visual processes from drawing or has a verbal etiology.

Shaughnessy (2000), in a study compared the effectiveness of two reading interventions in a public school setting. Forty-five second-grade children with reading disabilities were randomly assigned to a 6-week phonological awareness, word analogy or math-training program. The two reading interventions differed from each other in (a) the unit of word analysis (phoneme versus onset/rime); (b) the approach to intervention (contextualized versus decontextualized); and (c) the primary domain of reading instruction (oral versus written language). Results indicated that children in both reading programs achieved significant gains in beginning reading skills, learning the specific skills taught in their respective programs and applying what they had learned to uninstructed material on several transfer-of-learning measures, in comparison to children in the control group. For children in both reading intervention groups, the most significant mediator of growth in oral reading fluency was a child's initial level of word identification skill.

Arwood (2005), evaluated the effects of a reading intervention on the reading achievement and social behaviours of 6 third-grade students with emotional/behavioural disorders. Reading instruction occurred 4 days a week using the Horizons Fast Track reading program and Peer-Assisted Learning Strategies. Analyses indicated variable improvements in basic reading skills with limited transfer to oral reading fluency. Outcomes for social behaviours indicated that changes in total inappropriate behaviour were not directly related to the reading intervention; improved engagement appeared related to intervention but not necessarily reading achievement.

Michal (2011), investigated that the extent to which children's knowledge about reading disabilities, preoccupation with their own reading disability, and anxiety predicted reading comprehension in fifth and sixth grade children with reading disabilities (N = 85). Participants provided rich and accurate information about reading disabilities and the academic and emotional implications of having a reading disability. Children's knowledge about the characteristics of reading disabilities was positively associated with reading comprehension, and pre-occupation with their own disability was negatively associated with reading comprehension. Girls reported higher levels of pre-occupation and anxiety than boys did. In addition to gender, children's reading comprehension, trait anxiety, and perceptions of their mothers' worry about their reading disabilities predicted their pre-occupation with their own disability. Children with the most adaptive profile in terms of reading comprehension and anxiety were those who had high levels of knowledge and low levels of pre-occupation with their disability.

(b) Writing Problem

Stanley and Leonard (2001), explored the experiences of children with learning disabilities, with a focus on the day-to-day activities of reading and writing at school. Eight children, aged nine to thirteen were interviewed, from three to six sessions each. A phenomenological interviewing and interpretation process was undertaken, and common experiences among the children were extracted from the interview transcripts. Their common experiences included feeling more similar to than different from their peers, success in school subjects and other areas, progress in their literacy skills, enjoying literacy, teachers making a difference, not enough time, frustration, confusion, and corrupters making a difference. There appears to be some room for improvement in specific cases, to help reduce confusion, hesitation, and concerns about time limits, as well as increased attention to math and computer technology.

(c) Mathematics

Michele and Myers (2003), reported findings from a prospective longitudinal study of math disability (MD). The study was designed to address the incidence of MD during primary school, the utility of different MD definitions, and evidence of MD subtypes. The results highlighted the complexities of defining MD and the author felt that there is a need for more research in this area.

(d) Language Problems

Vallance (2001), focused on developmental-organizational perspective to explore underlying risk for problem behaviour in children with language learning disabilities. The independent and relative influences of social discourse and social skills on problem behaviour were examined in 50 children with language learning disabilities (LLD) and 50 control children (children without LLD) aged 8 to 12 years. Hierarchical regression analyses revealed that when examined independently, both impaired social discourse skill and poor social skills accounted for the negative effect of LLD status on children's problem behaviour. Differences were confirmed in social discourse performance, social skills, and problem behaviours between the children with LLD and the control group children.

While the previous study deals with math disability, the study conducted by Vallance (2001), was on problem behaviour of children with language learning disability.

(e) Academic Difficulties

Rogers and Saklofske (1985), examined general and academic self-concepts, general and academic locus of control beliefs and academic performance expectations among 45 learning disabled (LD) and 45 normally achieving (NA) children aged 7 years, 6 months to 12 years, 9 months. The LD children were significantly different from the NA children on the set of affective variables and on each of the individual variables. The LD children had lower self-concepts, more external locus of control orientations and lower performance expectations. LD children newly enrolled in resource room programs (NLD) were significantly different from LD children with more than six months of experience in such programs (ELD) on the set of affective variables. However, the only individual variable to significantly differentiate these groups was academic performance expectation. The NLD children had higher expectations for future success than the ELD children. Among the affective variables, only general and academic locus of control and academic self-concept contributed significantly to the prediction of the extent to which the ELD children were academically successful (teacher-rated) in their special programs. The study provided some insights into the affective characteristics of LD children.

Lurae and Johnson (2008), conducted a study to determine whether an overall low average or a specific learning disability is a better predictor of a student displaying aggression at school. Further, the study explored interaction between an overall low average and a specific learning disability. The subjects were students in grades six through eight who attended a traditional middle school in a rural school. The subjects had been punished by an out-of-school suspension at least once for an act of aggression during the 2006-2007 school years'. Using a multiple regression analysis, the researcher found a negative correlation between overall average and suspensions for the number of aggressive acts displayed at school. As overall average decreased, the number of suspensions for acts of aggression increased. The presence of a specific learning disability label did not significantly correlate with aggression. Neither did the presence of both a low overall average and a specific learning disability label prove to be significant. When both factors were present for a subject, the low overall average was shown to be the more important correlate with aggression. The researcher concluded that an overall low average was a better predictor for the likelihood of a student displaying aggression at school than was a specific learning disability label.

(f) Mixed Problems

Vogel (1990), reviewed the research which confirmed higher verbal ability in normally achieving females and higher visual-spatial and mathematical abilities in normally achieving males. However, the specific nature of these differences varies by age, specific measure, magnitude, and variability within the groups. Re-analysis of earlier research showed that, although differences in visual-spatial ability were larger than verbal ability differences, gender differences did not account for more than 1% to 5% of the group variance. In the population with learning disabilities (LD), research must be interpreted cautiously because LD samples were drawn mainly from the system-identified population and may reflect selection bias. Findings indicate that system-identified females with LD are lower in IQ, have more severe academic achievement deficits in some aspects of reading and math, and are somewhat better in visual-motor abilities, spelling, and written language mechanics than males with LD. In mathematics, however, it is difficult to document consistent differences in computational skills in the elementary school ages.

Gathercole *et al.*, (2006), investigated associations between working memory (measured by complex memory tasks) and both reading and mathematics abilities, as well as the possible mediating factors of intelligence, verbal abilities, short-term memory (STM), and phonological awareness, in a sample of 46, 6- to 11-year-olds with reading disabilities. As a whole, the sample was characterized by difficulties in complex memory and visual spatial STM and by low IQ scores; language, phonological STM, and phonological awareness abilities fell in the low average range. Severity of reading difficulties within the sample was significantly associated with complex memory, language, and phonological awareness abilities, whereas poor mathematics abilities were linked with complex memory, phonological STM, and phonological awareness scores. These findings suggested that working memory skills indexed by complex memory tasks represent an important constraint on the acquisition of skill and knowledge in reading and mathematics.

The studies on to problems related to learning disabilities revealed the following points.

- Children's knowledge about the characteristics of reading disabilities was positively associated with reading comprehension, and pre-occupation with their own disability was negatively associated with reading comprehension.
- Children with LD reading programs achieved significant gains in beginning reading skills, learning the specific skills and applying what they had learned to uninstructed material on several transfer-of-learning measures, in comparison to children in the control group.

- Specific learning disability label did not significantly correlate with aggression.
- Both children with and without learning disability performed well on test of verbal intelligence but differed significantly on measures of reading achievement and visual.
- Artistic talent seemed to be co-exist with dyslexia. Dyslexia either involves different visual processes from drawing or has a verbal etiology.
- The LD children had lower self-concepts, more external locus of control orientations and lower performance expectations. LD children newly enrolled in resource room programs (NLD) were significantly different from LD children with more than six months of experience in such programs (ELD) on the set of affective variables.

Perceptions of Parents, Children and Teachers about Learning Disability

(a) Parental Perception of Learning Disability

Indian Study

In an Indian study, Chandramuki *et al.*, (2012), explored parental attitudes towards children with learning disabilities. The sample comprised parents of 60 children (30 boys and 30 girls) with specific learning disability who attend the child and adolescent psychiatry out-patient at National Institute of Mental Health and Neuroscience, Bangalore, India. The attitudes of parents were assessed using the parental attitude scale. The results revealed significant differences related to gender of the children on various domains of the scale. The study highlighted that there was a need to educate parents to lower their expectations for children with specific learning disability and to strengthen the social support network of the children's families.

Abroad Studies

Waggoner and Lorraine (1990) reported about the expression of concerns of the parents of children with LD about school isolation and future well being of their children with LD. The study revealed that majority of the parents of the LD children reported that teachers were uncooperative, unsupportive, inflexible and uninformed about their child's LD. These parents also indicated many emotional and physical strains from parenting such as lack of self esteem and more physical demands. Some of the parents also reported positive effects such as added strength in family life by adopting more values.

Same author along with Wilgosh discussed regarding parental involvement in children academics.

Waggoner and Wilgosh (1990), examined the experiences and concerns of a group of parents of children with learning disabilities. Parents of eight different families were interviewed in depth, and seven themes emerged from the interviews. Parents discussed their involvement in their child's education, and their positive and negative experiences with school personnel as well as with seeking other sources of support. They expressed concerns about the social isolation and future well-being of their children with learning disabilities. They indicated many emotional strains from parenting children with learning disabilities and that there are both positive and negative effects on the families.

Dorit (1991), examined the self-images of 49 adolescents with learning disabilities (Grades 9 through 12, mean age = 15.9) and 49 normally achieving peers (Grades 9 through 12, mean age = 16.0). The students were compared using the Offer Self-Image Questionnaire (OSIQ). The group with LD scored significantly lower than the comparison group on 4 of the 10 OSIQ scales. Later diagnosed adolescents with LD scored significantly higher than early-diagnosed adolescents on two of the scales. Severity of the learning disability was not found to be related to self-image scores. In a second study, parental perceptions of the self-images of 28 of the 49 students with LD were studied by administering the Offer Parent-Adolescent Questionnaire (OPAQ) and an informal questionnaire to their parents. On 6 of the 10 OPAQ scales, parents perceived their children as having a lower self-image than the adolescents themselves reported. Significant but moderate relationships were found between parents' perceptions and adolescent self-image scores.

Stephenson (1992), examined information about the attitudes and beliefs of mothers concerning their children in learning disabilities classes. Four mothers were interviewed over a 1-year period. Their comments about services provided by educational and mental health professionals indicated high levels of frustration and dissatisfaction. Parental expectations and perspectives differed from those of educators. Participants and educators were found to view learning disabilities differently.

Dyson (1996) compared quantitative and qualitative measures of 19 parents and 19 siblings of school-age children with learning disabilities and non disabled children and reported that parents in the former group experienced greater stress than did parents of nondisabled children. Learning disabilities are common conditions in pediatric patients. The etiology of these difficulties is multi factorial, reflecting genetic influences and abnormalities of brain structure and function. The author opined that early recognition and referral to qualified educational professionals is critical for the best possible outcome. Visual problems are rarely responsible for learning difficulties.

Chapman (1999), mentioned about Academic locus of control and mothers' school-related reactions and expectations were studied in 81 learning disabled (LD) and 81 normally achieving (control) children in Grades 3-6. The Intellectual Achievement Responsibility Questionnaire, the Intellectual subscale of the Parent Reaction Questionnaire, and the Parents Version of the Projected Academic Performance Scale were used. LD Subjects indicated more external perceptions of control with respect to successful academic experiences. For failure outcomes, no difference between LD and control children was found; however, a trend toward increased internality was noted over grade levels for both groups. Mothers of LD Subjects reported more negative and fewer positive reactions to their children. They also held lower academic performance expectations for their children than control mothers.

(b) Self Perception by Children

Wendy (1990), studied Eighty-seven children with learning disabilities, aged 9 through 11 years 11 months, completed measures of self-esteem, academic self concept, and self perception of their learning disability. The Self-Perception of Learning Disability (SPLD) instrument measures the extent to which children with learning disabilities perceive their disability as (a) delimited rather than global; (b) modifiable rather than permanently limiting; and (c) not stigmatizing. It was hypothesized that self-perception of one's learning disability would be related positively to both academic self-concept and self-esteem, and that each of these relationships would remain significant when controlling for sex, ethnicity, age, reading and math achievement, self-contained versus mainstreamed classroom setting, and age at diagnosis. Correlations and multiple regression analyses confirmed these hypotheses.

(c) Children and Teachers Perception

Strawderman and Watson (1992), focused on the Prevalence of Depressive Symptoms in Children with Learning Disabilities. The study examined the prevalence of depressive symptoms in a sample of public school elementary children aged 8 through 11, 37 boys and 16 girls, identified as LD by state standards. Of the sample of 53 children, 35.85 per cent scored in the depressed range on the Children's Depression Inventory. Comparison of the children's self-reports and parents' reports of depressive symptoms in their children were not significant.

- Most of the parents with LD had worries about their child's future, felt more guilt and embarrassment within the family, neighbors and school due to name callings and fights.
- Parents also indicated many emotional and physical strains from parenting such as lack of self esteem and more physical demands.
- Parental expectations and perspectives differed from those of educators. Parents and educators were found to view learning disabilities differently.

- There is a need to educate parents to lower their expectations for children with specific learning disability and to strengthen the social support network of the children's families.
- Mothers of LD Subjects reported lower academic performance expectations for their children than control mothers.
- Parents' indicated many emotional strains from parenting children with learning disabilities.
- Comparison of the children's self-reports and parents' reports of depressive symptoms in their children was not significant.

Management of Problems Related Learning Disability

Children with Special Education

Abroad Studies

Renick and Susan (1989), investigated learning disabled (LD) children's self-perceptions using the Perceived Competence Scale for Children. This self-report instrument taps children's perceptions of their scholastic and athletic competence, social acceptance, and feelings of global self-worth. Participants in the study were 86 students in Grades 3-8 who attended a public school LD resource room. Results indicated that social comparison processes play an important role in the formation of LD students' perceived academic competence. LD students perceived themselves as becoming less academically competent across the grade span tested when they compared themselves with normally achieving students in their regular classes. When children with LD compared their abilities with LD peers in their resource room, they maintained high perceptions of their own academic competence.

Webber and Scheuermann (1993), examined twenty-seven studies pertaining to the use of self-monitoring for behaviour management purposes in special education classrooms. The studies were described in detail, questions regarding the reactivity of self-monitoring were posited, and implications for classroom instruction were delineated. It was found that self-monitoring can be successfully used with special education students of various ages in various settings to increase (a) attention to task; (b) positive classroom behaviours; and (c) some social skill. It can also be successfully used to decrease in appropriate classroom behaviour. Self-monitoring apparently has the additional benefit of enhancing the likelihood that positive classroom behaviours will generalize to other settings. Self-monitoring techniques are easy to teach and have great promise as a behaviour management strategy.

Banerji and Ronald (1995),studied on the effects of an inclusion program in Grades 2 to 5 in a three-part study focusing, respectively, on the academic and affective outcomes of fifth-grade students who were normally achieving

(NA) or showed specific learning disabilities (SLD); teacher and parent perceptions of SLD and NA students' growth in an inclusion context for Grades 2 to 4; and an analysis of anecdotal records. Findings suggested that students with SLD made some academic and affective gains at a pace comparable to that of NA students; parent and teacher surveys indicated improved self-esteem in students with SLD, and, in some cases, improved motivation. Anecdotal data suggested reduced stigma for students with SLD.

Stephen and Robert (1997), conducted a study to determine whether learning disordered students (broadly defined) were afforded different interactions from their regular classroom teachers than were children achieving at low, medium, or high levels. The dyadic teacher-child interactions of 110 first-grade students in four classrooms in two middle-class, suburban schools were recorded for seven hours per week for the first 13 weeks of the school year. Data analysis revealed that learning disordered children received more teacher criticism in teachers with university based professional development appeared both to hold more positive attitudes and to be more confident in meeting the IEP requirements of students with SEN interactions concerning classroom procedures and more teacher criticism and warning regarding behaviour than their nondisabled peers. The authors concluded with the speculation that regular classroom teachers may be ill-equipped to manage the learning behaviour of learning disordered children.

Elias *et al.*, (2010), surveyed about attitudes of mainstream teachers towards the inclusion of children with special needs in the ordinary school. The survey was carried out in one Local Education Authority in the south-west of England and the sample comprised of 81 primary and secondary teachers. The analysis revealed that teachers who have been implementing inclusive programmes, and therefore have active experience of inclusion, possess more positive attitudes. Moreover, the data showed the importance of professional development in the formation of positive attitudes towards inclusion.

Lisa *et al*,.(2010), investigated the state of inclusion practices in general education classrooms via survey of 71 inclusion teachers who served as special educators across the state of New York. Specifically, small group instruction, co-teaching, one-to-one instruction, and planning support are explored in relationship to class size, number of students with disabilities and severity of disability. The qualifications, strengths, and professional development experiences of inclusion teachers based on their reported years of teaching experience, preparatory course work, and professional development opportunities are examined. Finally, information on common forms of assistance including consultant special education teachers, teacher assistants, and classroom volunteers are documented. Quantitative analysis of survey responses indicated great variability among the inclusion practices employed in general education classrooms. Co-teaching, though frequently cited as the most beneficial model of inclusive practice, emerged as the least documented method of instruction, with the utilization of consultant teacher models emerging as the most prevalent. Endorsement of the use volunteer support was found to be the second most common support mechanism employed within inclusive classrooms. Few differences in the types of supports employed were found across population densities.

Regina and Scholte (2012), who compared the discriminating special needs characteristics of children with emotional and behavioural disorders (EBD) that predict restrictiveness of placement in special education. The focus is on dynamic factors instead of static factors. To this end, 235 children with EBD in special schools and 111 children with EBD in regular education were compared in terms of behavioural, emotional, academic, and environmental variables. Measurements used were the *Child Behaviour Checklist* and *Teacher's Report Form*, information in the children's assessment reports, and the *Dutch Family Home Environment Scale*. In a logistic regression analysis, eight variables were found to be relevant predictors for placement in special schools instead of regular education. Relational problems between child and caregiver, academic performance, and the age at which the child received care for the first time were identified as the three predictors that could most affect the inclusion of children with EBD in regular education.

The above studies were about inclusion of learning disability children in normal school below mentioned study is about resource room teachers

In one longitudinal analysis Elaine and Lucian (1996), focused on academic, social, and behavioural adjustment for students declassified from special education. Each year 7% of Michigan's special education students return to full-time general education programs through declassification. In a preliminary investigation of declassification from special education, the authors analyzed data collected by the Michigan Department of Education over the past 5 years. Respondents suggested that, as a group, students declassified from special education are academically, socially, and behaviourally well adjusted; but teachers or counselors of 11% of the declassified students felt that these students continued to require special education services. Within 3 years, 4% of declassified students had returned to special education. Particularly noteworthy were the relatively poor results for declassified students with emotional impairments.

Baum *et al.*, (1998), conducted a study to determine the prevalence of social dysfunction among students with learning disabilities as perceived by resource room teachers. The results indicate that up to 38% of this student population was in need of social skills intervention but that relatively few were actually receiving the needed interventions.

However, from student's perception all types of special education classes have their own preference which can be understood from a review by Vaughn and Klingner (1998).

Vaughn and Klingner (1998), analyzed and synthesized findings from eight studies that have examined the perceptions of students with learning disabilities of their educational settings described. Interviews and surveys with 442 students with learning disabilities yielded five overall findings:

1. The majority of students with learning disabilities preferred to receive specialized instruction outside of the general education classroom for part of the school day;
2. Students stated that they liked the resource room because the work is easier and fun and they get the help they need to do their work;
3. Students indicated that they liked the inclusion classroom because it was better for making friends;
4. Most students valued the support provided by the special education teacher in the general education classroom and did not know that he or she was the special education teacher; and
5. most students were unsure as to how they were placed in special education and who was responsible for the decision about whether they received special services in the general education classroom or the resource room.

The progress of learning disabled children can be achieved most through self monitoring or self regulation which is reported below.

In yet another study Vaughn along with Elbaum (1998), conducted a study on Social outcomes of students who participated in two different educational settings designed to provide special services for students with learning disabilities (LD) placed full-time within the general education classroom. Participants were 185 third through sixth-grade students: 59 students with LD, 72 low to average achieving, and 54 high achieving. There was an overall educational setting effect, with students on the consultation/collaborative teaching setting demonstrating more positive outcomes than students in the co-teaching setting on friendship quality and peer acceptance. Students with LD in the consultation/collaborative teaching setting also demonstrated moderate increases in the number of reciprocal friendships from fall to spring.

Barry (2004), evaluated the effects of four forms of progress monitoring on the oral reading rate of 48 elementary-age students with learning disabilities: teacher, peer, self and no-monitoring. Student progress toward long-term goals was measured twice weekly for 9 weeks, and participants were provided verbal and visual performance feedback. Analysis of group comparison data indicated no significant differences among conditions. Idiographic comparisons showed consistent gains across time for the teacher-monitor group and the largest gains from pretest to posttest for the self-monitor group. Furthermore, it was found that students in the self- and peer-monitoring conditions could collect reliable data on the number of correct words per minute. Teacher acceptability of the various procedures identified no significant differences for time or treatment. Student acceptability resulted in a significant effect for conditions.

Majority of students with learning disabilities preferred to receive specialized instruction outside of the general education classroom for part of the school day and students liked the resource room because the work is easier and fun and they get the help they need to do their work.

- Parent and teacher surveys indicated improved self-esteem in students with SLD and in some cases improved motivation.
- When children with LD compared their abilities with LD peers in their resource room, they maintained high perceptions of their own academic competence.
- Relational problems between child and caregiver, academic performance, and the age at which the child received care for the first time were identified as the three predictors that could most affect the inclusion of children with EBD in regular education.
- Up to 38% of this student population was in need of social skills intervention but that relatively few were actually receiving the needed interventions.
- Inclusive education of children with special needs in the ordinary school reported that to some extent inclusion is beneficial and it seems to be depend on teachers' professional development. The regular class room teacher seems to be ill equipped to manage the leaning disability children.
- LD students perceived themselves as becoming less academically competent across the grade span tested when they compared themselves with normally achieving students in their regular classes.
- A review of 27 studies revealed that the behaviour management of children in special education class rooms can be improved through teaching self monitoring techniques (Webber and Scheuermann, 1993).

Coping up of Problems related to Learning Disability

Indian Study

In an Indian study, Sunil, Rukshana and Madhuri (2011), reported that the management of specific learning disability (dyslexia, dysgraphia, and dyscalculia) afflicts 5-15% of school-going children. Over the last decade; awareness about this invisible handicap has grown in India. However, much needs to be done to ensure that each afflicted child gets an opportunity to achieve his or her full academic potential in regular mainstream schools. In order to achieve this ideal scenario, all 'regular' classroom teachers should be sensitized to suspect, and trained to screen for this disability when the child is in primary school. School managements should become proactive to set up resource rooms and employ special educators to ensure that these children receive regular and affordable remedial education; and be diligent in ensuring that these children get the mandatory provisions both during school and board examinations. The authors opined that once specific learning disability is recognized as a disability by the Government of India, these children with the backing of the Right to Education Act, would be able to benefit significantly.

Abroad Studies

In one study on adolescents, Cheryy and Joyce (1996), compared the experience of school-related stress during the transition to junior high school in a sample of 59 students with learning disabilities (27 females, 32 males) and 402 students without learning disabilities (241 females, 161 males). Using a checklist of 11 stressful school events, the authors found that adolescents with learning disabilities were more likely to report that they had failed a class and less likely to report they had been chosen for a school activity than their non-learning disabled peers. However, the two groups of students did not differ in their perceived stressfulness of any of the pertinent school events. Students with learning disabilities reported relying on cognitive avoidance as a coping strategy more heavily than did non-learning disabled students when coping with an academic stress event, and reported that they mobilized fewer peers for social support when dealing with an academic stressor or with an interpersonal problem. However, the sample students were adolescents.

Michal Al-Yagon (2007), examined the role of maternal personal resources (mother's attachment style, coping strategies, and affect) in moderating the effects of learning disabilities (LD) on children's socio emotional and behavioural adjustment (self-rated sense of coherence, loneliness, and hope; and mother-rated child behaviour checklist measures), as well as on their secure attachment among school-age children with LD. The sample consisted of 110 mother child dyads: 59 mothers and their children with LD (29 boys, 30 girls) and 51 mothers and their typically developing children (21 boys, 30 girls) from the same schools. Preliminary analyses indicated significant group differences on all children's measures and in several of the maternal personal resources. Mothers' low use of avoidant coping strategies and less avoidance in close relationships with significant others were found to moderate the effect of children's disabilities on children's level of loneliness, feelings of hope, and secure attachment.

In yet another study same author in 2011 reported on attachment with fathers as follows.

Michal Al-Yagon (2011), examined a cumulative model of vulnerability and protective factors at the individual level (children's attachment relationships with father and children's sense of coherence) and at the family level as manifested by fathers' coping resources (fathers' sense of coherence, fathers' active and avoidant coping strategies) in helping to explain differences in socio emotional and behavioural adjustment among children at the age 8 to 12 years with learning disabilities (LD) and or with typical development. The sample included 205 father-child dyads: 107 fathers and their children having LD and 98 fathers and their children with typical development, from the same public elementary schools. Preliminary analyses indicated significant group differences on all the children's measures as well as on fathers' avoidant coping strategies. Path analysis examined the multidimensional risk model for the LD and non-LD groups. The study found a high fit between the theoretical model and the empirical findings as well as a different pattern of relationship between the model's components for the two populations studied.

- With Individualized Remedial Education Plan (IEP) most children learn to cope with disability and may get integrated in a regular stream.
- Mothers' low use of avoidant coping strategies and less avoidance in close relationships with significant others were found to moderate the effect of children's disabilities on children's level of loneliness, feelings of hope, and secure attachment.
- Significant group differences on all the children's measures as well as on fathers' avoidant coping strategies.
- Mothers educational level will be unable to help in children's school work hence, delayer of diagnosis and remedial teachings.

The studies reviewed in this section have shown that adjustments of school children are primarily dependent on school variables, parental variables and family variables. The children with learning disability had problems in adjustments in areas like social, home, academic and emotional. Comparatively older children with LD showed more problems than younger ones. Studies have shown that boys with LD had significantly more behaviour problems than non learning disabled children.

Parents of children with disability experienced greater level of stress than these parents of children without disabilities. It was reported that prevalence of specific learning disability is increasing in Indian context also. In majority of cases mixed learning disability was reported.

Inclusive education of children with special needs is found to be beneficial for children and it depends up on the teachers' professional development. With individualized remedial education plan most children with LD learn to cope with disability and may get integrated in a regular stream.

The next chapter deals with the methodology.

3

Methodology

The major aim of the study was to understand the adjustment problems of children with learning disability in comparison with normal achievers based on parents' and teachers' perception. The scope of the study also includes the study of relationship among special education and adjustment problems and also coping up of problems by children with learning disability.

This chapter describes the research design of the study, tools and materials used to measure different variables used in the study, procedures employed in the construction and finalization of tools, mode of scoring the collected data and different statistical techniques employed in the analysis of data.

The study samples were children studying 3rd, 4th and 5th grades of elementary school age.

The research design shows the sample of the study and the tools administered to different sample groups.

The following are the variables of the present study:

Variables

1. *Child Variables* – Age
   Gender
   Birth order
   Grade/Class
   IQ
2. *Parent Variables* – Father's Educational Qualification
   Father's Occupation
   Mother's Educational Qualification
   Mother's Occupation

RESEARCH DESIGN

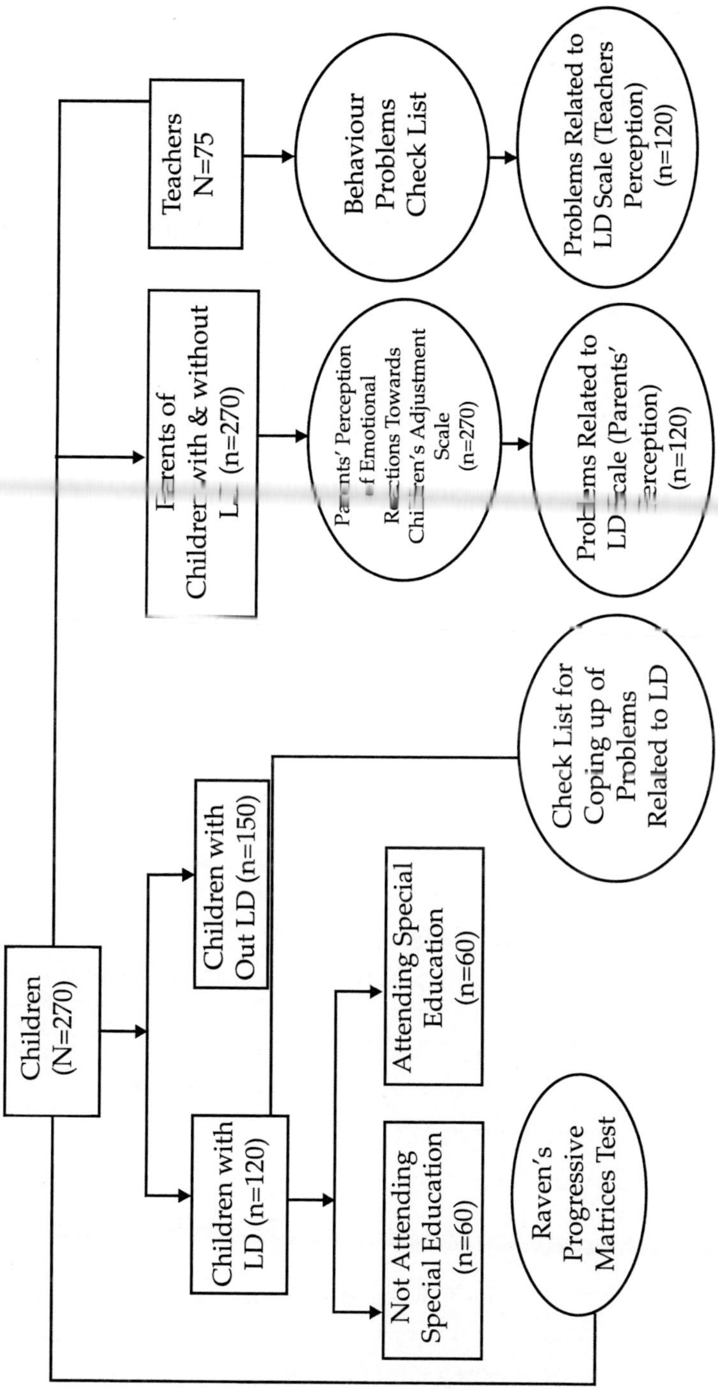

3. ***Family Variables*** – Type of family
   Income
4. ***LD variables*** – Type of LD (Listening, Speaking, Reading, Writing, Mathematics and Reasoning)
   Duration of LD Problem
5. ***Special Education Variables*** – Type of Special Education
   Duration of attending special education
   Time spends per day in special education classes
6. Parental Perception of Emotional Reactions towards Children's Adjustments
7. Teachers' Perception of Behaviour Problems of Children
8. Problems Related to Learning Disability
9. Coping up of Problems Related to Learning Disability from Children's Perspective

Tools and Materials for Research

For measuring the above mentioned different variables of the study the investigator developed three tools and two tools were adapted. The following are the tools developed/adapted to collect the information from three types of subjects that is Children (Normal achievers and children with learning disabilities), parents and teachers.

Tools Adapted

1. Learning Disability Diagnostic Inventory – (Developed by Hammill and Bryant 1998)
2. Standard Raven's Progressive Matrices (SRPM) Test (Developed by Raven, 1976)
3. Behaviour Problems Check List (Developed by Anuradha and Bharathi, 2004 and adapted for present study)

Tools Developed by the Investigator

4. General Information Schedule
5. Parental Perception of Emotional Reactions towards Children's Adjustments Scale.
6. Checklist for Problems Related to Learning Disability for Parents' and Teachers'.
7. Check List for Assessment of Coping up of Problems of Learning Disability.

The Tools developed for the present investigation were developed by following standard procedures for development of tools. The reliability and validity were established by testing the tools on a pilot study sample.

Pilot Study

A pilot study was conducted, on a sample of 50 children studying 3rd, 4th and 5th standard who were selected randomly from schools at Hyderabad and Tirupati. Ten schools were identified randomly from each place and 25 children with specific learning disability were identified using Learning Disability Diagnostic Inventory. Twenty five normal achievers were identified randomly from same classes from which LD were identified. The tools developed and adapted were administered on the pilot study sample. Item analysis was performed and the reliability was established using test-re test and split half reliability methods. The validity was established with help of judgment of experts from different fields like Child Development, Psychology and Special Education.

Description of Tools

Tools Adapted

1. Learning Disability Diagnostic Inventory (LDDI)

The tool was developed by Hammill and Bryant (1998). LDDI is an assessment device composed of items taken from the research and theoretical literature on Specific Learning Disabilities. The items represent specific observable behaviours associated with LD in Listening, Speaking, Reading, Writing, Mathematics and Reasoning. The scale helps to rate the Children's behaviours in the six areas, to summarize and profile each child's LDDI performance and to make diagnostic inferences based on the LDDI's results. The tool has 15 items in each component and in total 90 items.

Reliability

For this tool the reliability and validity were established by the authors. Reliability was established by three methods-content sampling, time sampling and scorer differences and the correlations were high to demonstrate acceptable reliability.

Validity

Validity was established through use of professional judgment and empirical procedures. Both reliability and validity of the tool established by the authors were satisfactory.

2. Raven's Progressive Matrices Test

The tool was developed by J.C.Raven, (1976). The test consists of five sets or series of diagrammatic puzzles exhibiting serial change in two dimensions simultaneously. Each puzzle has a part missing which the person taking the test has to find among the provided. The test consists of 60 problems divided into five sets (A, B, C, D and E), each made up of 12 problems. In each set the first problem is as nearly as possible self evident. The problems which follow build on the argument of those items provide the standard training in the method of working. The five sets provide five opportunities to grasp the method of thought required to solve the problems and five progressive assessments of a person's capacity for intellectual activity.

Reliability

For this tool the reliability and validity were established by the author. The test-retest reliability reported had higher reliability correlations.

Validity

The validity was established through criterion-oriented validity, predictive validity, content validity and factorial construct validity. The reliability and validity reported were satisfactory.

The Indian norms for the SPM of Raven's progressive Matrices were developed by Deshpande and Ojha (2002). The tool was found to be suitable for the study to assess the Intelligence Quotient of sample children.

3. Behaviour Problems Check List

The Check list for Children's Behaviour Problems was developed by the Bharathi and Anuradha (2004).

As per the authors the scale was categorized into 4 aspects like Home (11) Academic (10), Emotional (10) and Social (10) aspects.

Scoring

The procedure employed for scoring was as follows. The total numbers of problems in each area was obtained by counting all the items ticked. The intensity score for each area was counted by adding all the points given for each item on a response category ranging from 1 to 3. Thus, scores obtained for each subject, one for the total problems present and the other for its intensity.

Rationale

Higher the score indicate higher the behaviour problems reported by the respondents (Teachers and Parents), lesser score indicates less behaviour problems.

Reliability

The reliability for BPCL was established by the authors using test-retest method. Reliability co-efficient was calculated for each area of the check list i.e., Health (0.46), Emotional (0.72), Home (0.73), Leisure time/ Recreational activities (0.49), Academic (0.47) and peers (0.71).

Validity

The authors reported that the items selected for BPCL were based careful analysis by experts. The preliminary form was given to experts. An item which was agreed by at least three experts was included under each area. Thus, it can be said that the BPCL has 'content validity'.

Tools Developed

4. General Information Schedule

The General information schedule consists of general information about child age, ordinal position, School, and family particulars like type of Family and Members in the family etc.

5. Parental Perception of Emotional Reactions towards Children's Adjustments Scale (Developed by the Investigator)

Adjustment is a process by which a living organism maintains a balance between the needs and the circumstances.

The term adjustment is often used as a synonym for accommodation and adaptation. Strictly speaking, the term denotes the results of equilibrium, which may be affect by either of these processes (Monroe, 1990). It is used to emphasize the individual's struggle to along or survive in his or her social and physical environment.

Development of the Tool

The Parents' Perception of Emotional Reactions towards Children's Adjustments Scale was developed specially for present research purpose to assess the Parental Perception of Emotional Reactions towards Children's Adjustments.

Standardized tools like BPCL (Anuradha and Bharathi, 2004), Adjustment Inventory for School Children (Sinha and Singh, 1971) were referred for developing the tool. Different aspects of children's behaviour which causes stress to parents were gathered from related literature and also from teachers and parents. The items were classified under different sections as Home, School, Social and Emotional.

The statements regarding Parental Perception of Emotional Reactions towards Children's Adjustments were listed in four aspects viz., Home, Social, School and Emotional. Thus, the preliminary scale has four components – Home (20 items), school (16 items), Social (20 items) and Emotional (17 items) and in total there were 73 items. The typed schedule forms were given to experts from different fields and also to mothers of elementary school children with and without learning disabilities. They were requested to add any other statements and give suggestions for restructuring the Scale. Their suggestions were accepted and accordingly, the schedule was modified and re-arranged. Each statement was given a rating on five point scale as "Strongly Agree, Agree, Can't Say, Disagree and Strongly Disagree".

Only mothers of the selected children were administered with the tool. The first reason for selecting mothers was the practical difficulty of getting both the parents together. Fathers were available only either late in the evening or in holidays. It would have been time consuming to obtain information from both the parents. Secondly, it was felt that comparatively mothers perceive more stress about children's adjustments as mothers spend maximum time with children.

To examine the suitability of items included in the scale and to eliminate those which are not suitable and to rearrange if necessary, the tool was administered on pilot sample.

After conducted pilot study, Item analysis was performed.

Item Analysis

Item validity is generally determined by computing how well the item discriminates between two extreme groups. Extreme groups are set up on the basis of total scores. It is the practice to take the top 10 per cent and bottom 10 per cent. Each item will be examined to see whether it is able to separate the two groups. After conducting item analyses items with poor validity index were removed

The final form of the Parents' Perception of Emotional Reactions towards Children's Adjustments scale has 42 items and the distribution of items in different heads is as follows - Academic 12, home 12, Emotional 10 and Social 8.

Procedure for Administration of PPCAS

After establishing good rapport, the mothers were individually asked to recall and recognize any of the mentioned problems in the scale, as far as the selected child was concerned. Mothers was asked to indicate the answer with tick mark against each of such items and then they were also asked to mark for the intensity of occurrence (strongly agree, agree, can't say, Disagree and strongly disagree) of the aspects as far as their observation was concerned. With illiterate parents, the investigator herself read each item slowly and recorded their responses.

Depending on the type of statement, scoring was given. The expected minimum score was 42 and maximum was 210. The scoring procedure is shown in table 3.3.

Table 3.1

Scoring for Parental Perception of Emotional Reactions towards Children's Adjustment Problems

Sl. No.	Type of Statement	Scoring				
		SA	A	CS	D	SD
1.	positive	1	2	3	4	5
2.	Negative	5	4	3	2	1

Rationale

High score showed that parents were experiencing more stressful emotional reactions about Child's adjustments and a lower score indicated that parents were experiencing less stressful emotional reactions regarding their children's adjustment problems.

Reliability

The final form was again given to same parents sample after a gap of one month to establish test-retest Reliability. The reliability coefficient was 0.723 and it was found be significant.

Validity

The items selected for PPCAS were based on careful analysis by experts. The preliminary form was given to experts. An item which was agreed to by at least three experts was included under each area. Thus, it can be said that the PPCAS has 'Content Validity'.

6. Checklist for Problems Related to Learning Disability (For Parents and Teachers)

The Checklist for Problems Related to Learning Disability was developed by the investigator by following standard procedures for development of tool. The tool was developed to collect data only from the parents and teachers of sample who were identified as having LD.

Development of the Tool

Different areas which cause more problems to parents and teachers of children with Learning Disability were identified. Information was gathered from related literature, teachers and parents also. The items in each section were listed, sorted and rewritten wherever necessary and organized in to 16areas. Experts were selected from the fields of Special Education, Human Development and Psychology. The typed schedule forms were given to experts and mothers and teachers of elementary school children with learning disabilities. They were requested to add any other statements or eliminate the irrelevant statements if any, and give suggestions for restructuring the Schedule.

Their suggestions were accepted and accordingly, the schedule was modified and rearranged. The statements were developed as a check list for respondents to answer on a three point scale ranging from 'Always, Some times and Never'.

The tool has two sections. Section I consists of information related to learning disability problems, age of identification of problem, particulars about special education etc.

Section II has 11 problem areas like Reading problems, Writing problems, Mathematical problems, Syntax and Language problems, Visual perception problems, Auditory perception problems, Visual reception problems, Auditory reception problems, Directional confusion, Attention problems and Academic achievement respectively. The preliminary form was administered on the sample for pilot study. The items which were not checked by at least 20 per cent were deleted and the final form of scale and the scale was translated into Telugu regional language.

Procedure for Administration CPRLD

After establishing good rapport, the mothers were individually asked to recall and recognize any of the mentioned problems in the scale, as far as the selected child was concerned. Mothers was asked to indicate the answer with tick mark against each of such items and then they were also asked to mark for the intensity of occurrence (strongly agree, agree, can't say, Disagree and strongly disagree) of the aspects as far as their observation was concerned. With illiterate parents, the investigator herself read each item slowly and recorded their responses. The parent went through the entire list of items slowly and responded to the each question marking each item 'Always, Some times and Never'.

Scoring

The procedure employed for scoring was as follows, the total number of problems in each area was obtained by counting all the items ticked. The intensity score for each area was counted by adding all the points given for each item on a response category ranging from 1 to 3.

Depending on the type of statement, scoring was given. The expected minimum score was 6 and maximum was 18 in each component.

Rationale

High score showed that parents and teachers perceived more problems related to LD and vice versa.

Reliability

The final form was again given to same parents sample after a gap of one month to establish test – retest Reliability. The reliability coefficient was 0.5102 and it was found be significant.

Validity

The items selected for PPCAS were based on careful analysis by experts. The preliminary form was given to experts. An item which was agreed to by at least three experts was included under each area. Thus the checklist developed has 'content validity'.

7. Check list for Assessment of Coping up of Problems of Learning Disability (Developed by the Investigator)

Neuropsychological differences can impact the accurate perception of social cues with peers. A diagnosis of a learning disability can be potentially devastating to an individual and their family. Both the individual and their family need to learn methods of coping with the effects of the disorder; they also need to learn how to cope with the disorder emotionally. Stress related to the disorder can accumulate, making the coping process difficult. Stigmas that friends/family/peers have about the learning disorder can also contribute to the stress level the individual feels. Learning disabilities are often present throughout the lifespan, so learning appropriate and effective methods of coping are essential to successful management of the disorder.

The Check list for Assessment of Coping up of Problems of Learning Disability was developed by the investigator by following standard procedures for development of check list.

Development of the Tool

Items related to general problems of children with LD and were categorized into 4 aspects like Home, School/Academic, Emotional and Peer Aspects. The items were framed in the areas of coping up by children and thus a preliminary form with 55 items were framed and the preliminary form of check list. The same sample of children with LD studying 3rd, 4th and 5thgrades in elementary schools and special schools who were identified for pilot study was administered with the tool.

The suitability of items included in the schedules were examined and those which are not suitable and were rearranged if necessary after administering on the sample for pilot study. The items which were not checked by at least 20 per cent were deleted and the final form of scale and the scale was translated into Telugu regional language.

Procedure for Administration CCSCPLD

After establishing good rapport, each child with LD was interviewed separately in a room or in some privacy place in the school premises, in order to collect the information about their coping up of problems related LD. The child went through the entire list of items slowly and responded to the each question marking each item 'Yes', 'No' and 'Can't say'.

The procedure employed for scoring was as follows, the total number of problems in each area was obtained by counting all the items ticked. The intensity score for each area was counted by adding all the points given for each item on a response category ranging from 1 to 3.

Scoring

Table 3.2

Scoring for Coping up of Problems by Children

Sl. No.	Type of Statement	Scoring		
1.	Positive	3	2	1
2.	Negative	1	2	3

Rationale

Higher score represent good coping up of problems and less score indicate that less coping up of problems.

Reliability

The final form was again given to same parents sample after a gap of one month to establish test – retest Reliability. The reliability coefficient was 0.6329 and it was found be significant.

Validity

The items selected for PPCAS were based on careful analysis by experts. The preliminary form was given to experts. An item which was agreed to by at least three experts was included under each area. Thus the checklist developed has 'content validity'.

Sample

The sample of learning disability children were identified using Learning Disability Diagnosis Inventory (LDDI, Hammill and Bryant 1998). From the Government schools 60 children with LD were identified purposively. The normal achievers were selected from same classes using stratified random sampling technique. Thus, 150 Normal achievers, 120 children with learning disability (60 children who were attending special education and 60 children who were not attending special education) constituted the sample. Mothers and teachers of the selected children were the sub-samples of the study.

Final Data Collection

The data was collected from children studying in 3rd, 4th and 5th grades in three places of state i.e., Hyderabad, Nellore and Chittoor Districts representing one district from different regions of the state i.e. Rayalaseema, Costal and Telangana. Five revenue divisions were selected randomly and total 15 revenue divisions among three districts were selected.

Table 3.3

Distribution of Sample Children without LD and With LD, According to Grade, District, and Type of SE

Grade	Chittoor				Nellore				Hyderabad				Total
	Without LD (Normal)	Children with LD			Normal	Children with LD			Normal	Children with LD			
		Attending SE		Not Attending SE		Attending SE		Not Attending SE		Attending SE		Not Attending SE	
		Resource Rooms	Full Time SE	–		Resource Rooms	Full Time SE	–		Resource Rooms	Full Time SE	–	
3rd	16 (10.7%)	1 (1.7%)	–	7 (11.7%)	14 (9.3%)	–	–	7 (11.7%)	20 ([illegible].3%)	3 (5.0%)	15 (25.0%)	7 11.7%)	90 (33.3%)
4th	20 (13.3%)	3 (5.0%)	–	7 (11.7%)	18 (12.05%)	3 (5.0%)	–	6 (10.0%)	20 ([illegible]3.3%)	2 (3.3%)	15 (25.0%)	9 (15.0%)	103 (38.1%)
5th	14 (9.3%)	1 (1.7%)	–	6 (10.0%)	18 (12.0%)	3 (5.0%)	–	6 (10.0%)	10 ([illegible].7%)	–	14 (23.3%)	5 (8.3%)	77 (28.5%)
Total	**50 (33.3%)**	**5 (8.3%)**	**–**	**20 (33.3%)**	**50 (33.3%)**	**6 (10.0%)**	**–**	**19 (31.7%)**	**50 ([illegible]3.3%)**	**5 (8.3%)**	**44 (73.3%)**	**21 (35.0%)**	**270 (100.0%)**

Within each revenue division 4 schools were selected randomly and then from each school children with learning disabilities were selected purposively. In the first stage with the help of school teacher students in 3rd, 4th and 5th grades who were backward in academics were administered with LDDI inventory. Based on the number of students with Learning disability available in each section double the number of normal achievers from same class were selected randomly. Thus, 150 Normal achievers, 120 children with learning disability (60 children who were attending special education and 60 children who were not attending special education) constituted the sample. Mothers and teachers of the selected children were the sub-samples of the study.

The sample children's were given with Ravens Progressive Matrices by following the standard procedure for administration of the test in school premises in a separate room with comfortable seating position for the child to perform the test. It took nearly 20-30 minutes for children to perform Raven's Progressive Matrices Test. Children with Learning Disabilities were administered with the Check list for Assessment of Coping up of Problems of Learning Disability on the same day during afternoons. It took nearly 15-20 minutes for children to answer the check list.

The teachers of selected classes were asked to rate the behaviour of children using Behaviour Problems Checklist and teachers of selected LD children were asked to rate Checklist for Assessment of Problems Related to Learning Disability.

Later the house addresses of children were collected from school records and the schedules of Parents' Perception of Emotional Reactions Towards Children's Adjustments were administered to parents' (n=270) and Checklist for Assessment of Problems Related to Learning Disability were administered for parents (120) of children with LD after establishing good rapport. It took nearly 15-20 minutes for parents to answer the check list.

Next chapter reveals about results and discussion.

4

Results and Discussion

The data collected from three groups of sample that is children without LD, children with LD attending special education and children with LD not attending special education were scored. Coding was given to the data. The data was subjected to vigorous analysis by using relevant statistical techniques. The nature of the analysis was determined from the point of view of the objectives formulated.

The following scheme has been applied for the statistical analysis of collected data, keeping in view, the general assumptions underlying the study and the nature, composition and characteristics of the data obtained:

- Tabulation of data to high-light the personal profile of the sample over demographic variables, family variables, learning disability variables, behaviour problems and emotional reactions of parents towards children's adjustments, special education variables, and coping up of problems by children.
- Application of appropriate tests of significance to see significant difference and association between independent and dependent variables and to study the impact of independent variables on the dependent variables.
- Application of multiple linear regression analysis to predict the significant contributors of behaviour problems, adjustments and coping up of problems by children.

Efforts were made to present and discus the results systematically in different sections for the purpose of clarity, convenience and ease for discussion as under:

Section I: Explains descriptive analysis about the personal, demographic variables of children, parents and family variables of normal achievers (Children without learning disability) and children with learning disability. This section also includes behaviour problems of children as per teacher's perception and parental perception of emotional reactions towards children's adjustments.

Section II: Consists ofgeneral information about LD variables, problems related to LD as per both teachers' and parents' perception and details about coping up of problems by children with LD. This section also explains about general information of Special education variables.

Section III: Deals with the demographic variables and behaviour problems among children with and without LD. This section also includes relationship between demographic variables and parental perception of emotional reactions towards children's adjustments.

Section IV: Explains relationship among LD variables and SE variables with behaviour problems and parental perception of emotional reactions towards children's adjustments.

Section V: Deals with the analysis of SE variables, problems related to LD and coping up of problems.

Section VI: Consists ofdeterminants of outcome variables, viz., behaviour problems of children, parental perception of emotional reactions towards children's adjustments and coping up of problems by children with LD.

As described the following is the out lay of results and discussion.

SECTION I

General Profile of the Sample (N=270)

Demographic Variables

(a) *Child variables*

(b) *Parent variables*

(c) *Family variables*

Behaviour Problems among Children (As per Teachers'Perception)

Parental Perception of Emotional Reactions towards Children's Adjustments

SECTION II

Learning Disability and Special Education Variables

Learning Disability Variables (n=120)

General Information about LD Variables

Problems Related to LD (As per Teachers' Perception)

Problems Related to LD (As per Parents' Perception)

Correlation of Problems Related LD between Parents' and Teachers' Perception

Coping up of Problems by Children with LD

Special Education Variables (n = 60)

General Information about SE Variables

SECTION III

Relationship of Demographic Variables with Behaviour Problems and Parents' Perception of Emotional Reactions towards Children's Adjustments

Demographic Variables and Behaviour Problems

Mean difference in Behaviour problems of children with and without LD

Child variables and Behaviour Problems among Children with and without LD

Demographic Variables and Parents' Perception of EmotionalReactions towards Children's Adjustments

Mean Difference in Parents' Perception of Emotional Reactions towards Children's Adjustments

Child variables and Parents' Perception of Emotional Reactions about Children's Adjustments

Parent variables and Parents' Perception of Emotional Reactions about Children's Adjustments

Family variables and Parents' Perception of Emotional Reactions about Children's Adjustments

SECTION IV

Relationship of LD and SE variables with Behaviour Problems and Parental Perception of Emotional Reactions towards Children's Adjustment

LD variables

LD Variables and Behaviour Problems

LD Variables and Parents' Perception of Emotional Reactions about Children's Adjustments

SE Variables

SE Variables and Behaviour Problems

SE Variables and Parents' Perception of Emotional Reactions towards Children's Adjustments

SECTION V

Analysis of SE Variables, Problems related to LD and Coping up of Problems.

Mean differences in Problems related to LD

SE Variables and Problems Related to LD

Mean Difference in Coping up of Problems by Children

SE Variables and Coping up of Problems by Children

SECTION VI

Determinants of outcome Variables

Determinants of Behaviour Problems of Children

Determinants of Parents' Perception of Emotional Reactions towards Children's Adjustments

Determinants of Coping up of Problems by Children with LD

Contribution of LD Variables towards Coping up of Problems by Children

Contribution of SE variables towards Coping up of Problems by Children

Results

The data collected from three groups of sample that is children without LD, children with LD attending special education and children with LD not attending special education were tabulated and discussed against reported literature in the following sections.

SECTION I

In this section descriptive analysis about the personal, demographic variables of children, parents, family of normal achievers (Children without learning disability) and children with learning disability are described. This section also includes behaviour problems of children as per teacher's perception and parental perceptions of emotional reactions towards children's adjustments.

General Profile of the Sample (N=270)

Demographic Variables: *The demographic variables discussed were child variables, parent's variables and family variables*

Child variables

The child variables of the study were grade, gender, age, birth order and Intelligence Quotient (IQ) of the child.

Table 4.1 shows the distribution of sample children with and without LD according to child variables. The sample constituted three groups of children i.e., children without LD (Normal Achievers), children with learning disability attending Special Education classes (LD 'with SE) and children with Learning Disability not attending Special Education (LD without SE). To get an overview of three groups of children across demographic variables, the data pertaining to three groups is presented in tables. Nevertheless, while discussing the results of data related to section I, the comparison between children with and without LD is highlighted.

Table 4.1

Distribution of Sample Children with and without LD according to Child Variables (Percentages in Parentheses)*

Sl. No.	Variables	Children Without LD) (Normal Achievers)	Children with LD			Grand Total
			Attending SE	Not Attending SE	Total Children with LD	
1.	**Grade**					
	3rd	50 (33.3)	19 (31.7)	21 (35.0)	40 (33.3)	90 (33.3)
	4th	58 (38.7)	23 (38.3)	22 (36.7)	45 (37.5)	103 (38.1)
	5th	42 (28.0)	18 (30.0)	17 (28.3)	35 (29.2)	77 (28.5)
2.	**Gender**					
	Boys	70 (46.7)	41 (68.3)	36 (60.0)	77 (64.2)	147 (54.4)
	Girls	80 (53.3)	19 (31.7)	24 (40.0)	43 (35.8)	123 (45.6)
	Total	150	60	60	120	
3.	**Age**					
	8 Years	43 (28.7)	15 (25.0)	20 (33.3)	35 (29.2)	78 (28.9)
	9 Years	37 (24.7)	15 (25.0)	20 (33.3)	35 (29.2)	72 (26.7)
	10 Years	39 (26.0)	15 (25.0)	13 (21.7)	28 (23.3)	67 (24.8)
	11 Years	31 (20.7)	15 (25.0)	7 (11.7)	22 (18.3)	53 (19.6)
4.	**Birth Order**					
	First	61 (40.7)	8 (13.3)	43 (71.1)	51 (42.5)	112 (41.5)
	Second	75 (50.0)	26 (43.3)	16 (26.7)	42 (35)	117 (43.3)
	Third/Fourth	14 (9.3)	26 (43.3)	1 (1.7)	27 (22.5)	41 (15.2)
5.	**IQ**					
	Below Average	27 (18.0)	22 (36.6)	6 (10.0)	28 (23.3)	55 (20.4)
	Average	93 (62.0)	31 (51.6)	43 (71.7)	74 (61.6)	167 (61.8)
	Above Average	30 (20.0)	7 (11.6)	11 (18.3)	18 (15.0)	48 (17.7)

* Same notation is followed throughout the report.

The sample for children with Learning Disability (LD) were selected using Learning Disability Diagnosis Inventory (LDDI, Hammill and Bryan 1998). Thus, 40 children (33.3 per cent) from 3rd grade, 45 children (37.5 per cent) from 4th grade and 35 children (29.2 per cent) from 5th grade, constituted the sample. Nearly an equal number of children without learning disability were identified from same classes to enable comparison (33.3 per cent from 3rd grade, 38.7 per cent from 4th grade and 28 per cent from 5th grade.

The sample children were selected from 3rd, 4th and 5th grades because it is most suitable age for early identification and intervention through proper remedial strategy for children with LD. Kavitha *et al.*, (2012), also reported second and third grade is most suitable to intervene through proper remedial strategies for children with LD. Hence, children studying in 3rd, 4th and 5th grades were selected for early identification and to facilitate remedial strategies by parents and teachers.

Among the samples who were identified as learning disabled, there were 64.22 per cent of boys and 35.8 per cent of girls. From the data it was evident that comparatively the prevalence of learning disability was more among boys than girls. These findings were in line with that of Smith (2004), who found that boys were 1.5 times more likely to be identified as LD than girls. Eme (1992), also reported that gender ratio in LD is 3.5 to 5 males for one female.The reasons for gender difference in prevalence of LD can be understood from the studies of Green *et al.*, (1996) and Shaywitz *et al.*, (1990), who reported that the reasons may be that boys tend to have more externalizing problems and social expectations and for girl's academic learning were not consistently high. Shaywitz *et al.*, (1990) reported that girls exhibit more passive behaviours such as sitting and daydreaming. So they are less likely to be identified as LD than boys.

The mean age of sample children without LD was 9.38 (SD 1.121) and for children with Learning disability the mean age was 9.30 (SD 1.127).

With regard to birth order of children, majority of normal achievers (50 per cent) were second born, next to it 40.7 per cent were first born and very few (9.3 per cent) sample children without LD had birth order of third and above. With regard to sample children with LD majority (42.5 per cent) were first born followed by second (35 per cent) and later born (27 per cent).

Studies have shown that with increase in number of siblings there is a decrease in number of positive cases of LD. Akhil and Tushar (2013) also reported that LD was more prevalent among first born children than later born.

Children's IQ was measured using Raven's Progressive Matrices Test (Raven 1976). From the table 4.1, it is clear that majority of sample children (62 per cent) without LD (Normal Achievers) had average intelligence quotient. Twenty per cent of NA fell under above average and an equal per cent (18 per cent) fell under bellow average IQ category.

It is interesting to note that on par with normal achievers majority of children with LD (61.6 per cent) had average intelligence and 23.3 per cent had below average intelligence. 15 per cent of children with LD were found to have above average intelligence.Miglani *et al.,* (2011) also found that there was no significant difference in intelligence among children with learning disability and non learning disability.

Studies have shown that people with learning disabilities have average to above average intelligence (Gerber. 1998, Sheema and Anamika. 2012), that may be the reason usually LD children were identified when they score less academic achievement than their intelligence.

Parent Variables

Parental variables of the study were father's education, Father's occupation and Mother's education and Mother's occupation.

Table 4.2 shows the distribution of sample children with and without LD according to their fathers' education and their occupation.

Table 4.2

Distribution of Sample Children with and without LD according to Fathers' Education and Occupation (Percentage in Parenthesis)

S.No.	Parental Variables	Children without LD (Normal Achievers)	Children with LD		
			Attending SE	Not Attending SE	Total Children with LD
1.	**Fathers'Education**				
	Illiterate	29 (19.3)	25 (41.7)	19 (31.7)	44 (36.67)
	Up to 10th Class	79 (52.7)	22 (36.7)	3 (5.0)	25 (20.8)
	Intermediate and above	42 (28.0)	13 (21.7)	38 (63.3)	51 (42.5)
2.	**Fathers' Occupation**				
	Daily labour	30 (20.0)	19 (31.7)	4 (6.7)	23 (19.17)
	Govt./private employee	33 (22.0)	11 (18.3)	16 (26.7)	27 (22.5)
	Business	55 (36.7)	14 (23.3)	12 (20.0)	26 (21.67)
	Agriculture and others	32 (21.3)	16 (26.7)	28 (46.7)	44 (36.7)

An observation of table 4.2 shows that the majority of fathers (52.7 per cent) of children without LD had education up to 10th standard and had occupation of business and Government employment. Majority of fathers of children with LD (42.5 per cent) had Intermediate and above education and 36.7 per cent were illiterates and with regard to occupation 36.7 per cent from agriculture back ground and other occupations like drivers, tailors etc.

Table 4.3 shows the distribution of sample according to mothers' education and occupation.

Table 4.3

Distribution of Sample according to Mothers' Education and Occupation

S. No.	Variables	Children without LD (Normal Achievers)	Children with LD		Total Children with LD	Grand Total
			Attending SE	Not Attending SE		
1.	**Mothers'Education**					
	Illiterate	21 (14.0)	30 (50.0)	14 (23.3)	44 (36.7)	65 (24.1)
	Up to 10th class	101 (67.3)	24 (40.0)	9 (15.0)	33 (27.5)	134 (49.6)
	Intermediate and above	28 (18.7)	6 (10.0)	37 (61.7)	43 (35.8)	71 (26.3)
2.	**Mothers'Occupation**					
	House wife	119 (79.3)	32 (53.3)	36 (60.0)	68 (56.67)	187 (69.3)
	Daily labour	4 (2.7)	12 (20.0)	4 (6.7)	16 (13.3)	20 (7.4)
	Govt./Private employee	11 (7.3)	8 (13.3)	8 (13.3)	16 (13.3)	27 (10.0)
	Business	6 (4.0)	5 (8.3)	6 (10.0)	11 (9.17)	17 (6.3)
	Agriculture/Others	10 (6.7)	3 (5.0)	6 (10.0)	9 (7.5)	19 (7.0)

From table 4.3, it is known that majority of mothers of children without LD (67.3 per cent) had education up to 10thstandardwhereas, majority of mothers of children with LD (36.7 per cent) were illiterates. With regard to occupation majority of mothers of children with LD and without LD were home makers and next to it, mothers of children of LD (13.3 per cent) were daily labours.

Paul *et al.*, (1990), also reported that mothers'low educational qualification and low occupational status (as daily labour) were significant risk factor for learning disability among children.

Carlson (1987), found that majority of the parents of LD children had lower educational attainment.

Wilson (1975) discovered that parental indulgence and infrequent punishment were associated with academic difficulties. Rezique (1983) found that mother's educational level influenced children's academic achievement. Parents with poor educational levels may lack motivation and academic ambition, be unable to help in their children's schoolwork and may have a low index of suspicion of their learning disabilities, delaying diagnosis and remedial teaching. Therefore the onus of identification of children with learning disability lies with teachers especially for those children whose mothers were illiterates and home makers.

Family Variables

Family variables of the study were type of family, family size and family income.

Table 4.4 shows the distribution of sample children with and without LD according to family variables.

Table 4.4

Distribution of Sample Children with and without LD According to Family Variables

S. No.	Family Variables	Children without LD (Normal Achievers)	Children with LD		Total Children with LD
			Attending SE	Not Attending SE	
1.	**Type of Family**				
	Nuclear	135 (90.0)	51 (85.0)	55 (91.7)	106 (88.3)
	Joint	15 (10.0)	7 (11.7)	5 (8.3)	12 (10.0)
	Extended	0 (0.0)	2 (3.3)	0 (0.0)	2 (1.67)
2.	**Family Size**				
	Up to 3 members	12 (8.0)	2 (3.3)	1 (1.7)	3 (2.5)
	4-6 Members	134 (89.3)	45 (75.0)	58 (96.7)	103 (85.83)
	7 and Above	4 (2.7)	13 (21.7)	1 (1.7)	14 (11.67)
3.	**Income Level**				
	Rs. 5000-10000/-	18 (12.0)	15 (25.0)	1 (1.7)	16 (13.33)
	Rs. 10000-15000/-	107 (71.3)	29 (48.3)	18 (30.0)	47 (39.17)
	Above Rs. 15000/-	25 (16.7)	16 (26.7)	41 (68.3)	57 (47.5)

From table 4.4 it is evident that majority of sample children, both children without LD (90 per cent) and children with LD (88.3 per cent) were from nuclear families. 10 per cent were from joint families and very few were from extended families. In majority of the families (89.3 per cent without LD and 85.83 per cent with LD), the number of family members were ranged from 4-6 members.

This clearly shows the changing Indian family structure of moving from joint to nuclear families.

With regard to monthly income, majority of normal achievers (71.3 per cent) were from families whose monthly income was Rs. 10000-15000/-. Among children with LD majority 47.5 per cent were from families whose monthly income was above Rs. 15000/- and 39.17 per cent were from families with income range of Rs. 10,000 to 15,000/-. The sample were selected from government schools in all three districts and hence,majority of the sample were from middle income group.

Venugopal and Raju (1988) also reported that children belonging to middle class families represented more learning disabilities.

Behaviour Problems among Children (As per Teachers' Perception)

Behaviour problems of children were assessed by teachers using Behaviour Problems Checklist (Anuradha and Bharathi, 2004). Teachers checked the behaviour problems exhibited by the children in four areas namely Home, Academic, Emotional and Social areas.Higher the score indicates more behaviour problems and vice versa.

Table 4.5 reveals the distribution of sample children with and without LD according to behaviour problems.

Table 4.5

Mean Scores for Behaviour Problemsof Sample Children with and without LD (As per Teachers' Perception)

Areas of Problems	Children without LD (Normal Achievers)		Children with LD				Total Children with LD	
			Attending Special Education		Not Attending Special Education			
	Mean	SD	Mean	SD	Mean	SD	Mean	SD
Emotional	13.36	4.057	21.35	5.698	22.03	3.78	21.69	4.83
Home	12.71	4.036	19.93	6.308	24.40	3.867	22.17	5.672
Academic	13.39	4.458	22.73	5.236	23.07	3.883	22.90	4.593
Social	12.57	4.017	17.15	5.281	24.00	3.613	20.58	5.668
Total	52.04	13.780	81.08	17.846	95.53	11.663	87.31	16.261

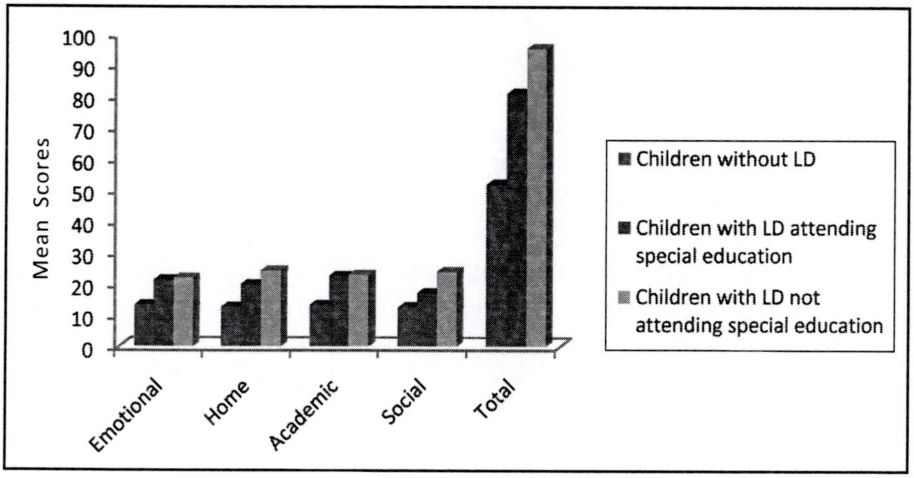

Fig 4.1: Mean Scores of Behaviour Problems for Children with and without LD in Four Areas of Adjustments

It divulges from table 4.5 and figure 4.1 that children without LD had more problems in academic (mean= 13.39; SD=4.458) and emotional areas (mean=13.36; SD=4.057) followed by home (mean 12.71 ; SD 4.036) and social areas (mean 12.57; SD 4.017). Whereas, for children with LD the teachers perceived more problems in academic (mean 22.90; SD 4.593) and home areas (mean 22.17; SD 5.672). Next to it, children had problems in emotional (mean 21.69 SD 4.83) and social areas (mean 20.58; SD 5.668). Comparatively children with LD seemed to have higher score in all areas of problem behaviour than those without LD according to teacher's perception, which indicates more problem behaviour among children with LD.

Reported studies on behaviour problems of children with LD and without LD have shown that comparatively children with LD have more behaviour problems than without LD (Stephanie and David (1986), Juvonen and George (1992), Lardieri, Blaches and Swanson (2000),James (2002) and Michaels (2004). Paul (1990) also reported that students of LD have more behaviour problems as per teacher's rating. Valence (2001), also reported that there were significant difference in social skills and problem behaviour between children with and without learning disability.

As children with LD not attending special education classes exhibited more behaviour problems, there is a need to motivate parents and teachers to make them attend special education classes.

Parental Perception of Emotional Reactions towards Children's Adjustments

The term 'adjustment' is often used as a synonym for accommodation and adaptation. It is used to emphasize the individual's struggle to get along with or survive in his or her social and physical environment.

Parents of elementary childrenhave many reactions to their children's adjustmentin areas like academic, home, emotional, social etc., and these reactions may focus on positive or negative factors. Some parents go through several emotions roughly in a sequence; others may experience only one or several discrete reactions. For some, the reactions may be minor and their approach pragmatic. For others, their child's disability might affect their entire family structure and life such as emotional stress and frustration.

When the child has to master skill in areas like academic, home, emotional, social etc., parents feel happy if the child is successful in making adjustments and they may be worried, experience stress and feel bad if their child could not compete with their peer groups. Hence, assessment of parental perception of emotional reaction towards their children adjustments has been selected as one of the variables of the study.

Adjustments of children from parents' perspective were assessed using Checklist for Parental Perception of Emotional Reaction towards Children Adjustments (CPPERCA). Higher the score on checklist indicates less stress for parents regarding children adjustments and vice versa.

Table 4.6 reveals the distribution of sample children with and without LD according to emotional reactions of parents towards children's adjustment problems.

Table 4.6

Mean Scoresfor Emotional Reactions of Parents towards Children's Adjustment of Children with and without LD

Areas of Problems	Children Without LD (NormalAchievers)		Children with LD					
			Attending Special Education		Not Attending Special Education		Total Children with LD	
	Mean	SD	Mean	SD	Mean	SD	Mean	SD
Academic	30.17	7.675	29.55	5.867	25.30	8.947	27.42	7.830
Home	30.37	6.308	28.73	7.818	23.75	8.446	26.24	8.481
Emotional	29.89	6.539	25.67	7.717	23.22	8.273	24.44	8.060
Social	28.41	5.815	21.37	6.265	19.22	7.402	20.29	6.913
Total	118.60	23.175	104.12	22.141	90.65	28.243	97.38	26.158

It is clearly known from table 4.6 and figure 4.2 that children without LD had more problems in social (mean 20.29; SD=6.91) and emotional (mean=24.4; SD=8.06) areas of adjustment followed by home and academic areas (mean=26.24; SD=8.48 and mean=27.42; SD=7.83). Whereas for children with LD the parent's perceived more problems in social (mean=28.41; SD=5.81) and emotional areas (mean=29.89; SD=6.54). Next to it, parents' perceived that children had problems in academic (mean=30.17; SD= 7.68) and home areas (mean=30.37; SD= 6.31). Comparatively children with LD seemed to have low score in all areas of adjustments than those without LD according to parent's perception. It indicated that parents of children with LD had more stress regarding their children's adjustments. These findings are in line with that of Dyson (2006), who also reported that parents of children with disabilities experienced a disproportionately grater level of stress relating to their children than did those of children without disabilities.

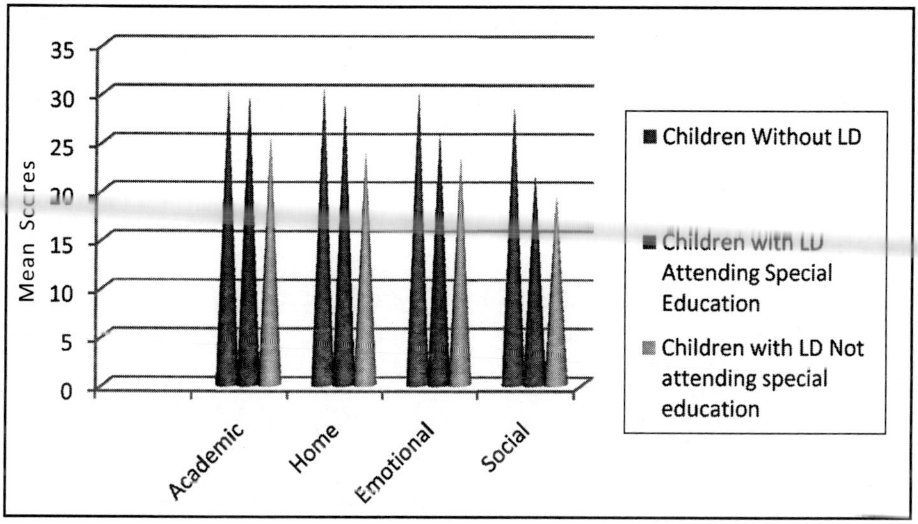

Fig. 4.2: Mean Scores of Parental Perception of Emotional Reactions towards Children's Adjustments

Parenting children with learning disabilities presents special challenges, not only with the child's everyday problems, but also with the associated social and emotional problems of school failure. Parents can be provided with skill training and emotional support to overcome stress related to learning disabilities of their children.

Doleys *et al.,* (1976) found that mothers of LD children think that their children had more behavioural and adjustment problems.

In an Indian study, Chandramuki *et al.,(*2012), explored about parental attitudes towards children with learning disabilities and found significant differences related to gender of the children on various domains of the scale. She opined that there was a need to educate parents to lower their expectations for children with specific learning disability and to strengthen the social support network of the children's families.

Dorit (1991), found that parents perceived that adolescents with LD had lower self image. Lower self-image may cause problems in social and emotional areas of adjustments for children.

Parental high expectations towards their children's achievement made them to experience more stress towards children's adjustments. As parents of children attending special education had comparatively less stress, education of parents to lower their expectations and creating awareness about special education helps to reduces negative emotional reaction towards children's adjustments.

SECTION II

In this section, general information about LD variables, problems related to LD as per both teachers' and parents' perception and details about coping up of problems by children with LD are explained. This section also explains about general information of Special education variables.

Learning Disability and SE Variables

Learning Disability

Learning disability, an unexplained difficulty experienced by children of at least average intelligence in acquiring basic academic skills usually identified during elementary school age.

Common problems of learning disabilities are listening, speaking, Reading, writing, mathematics and reasoning.

Table 4.7

Distribution of Sample according to Type of Problem across Status of Attending SE (Percentages in Parentheses)

Types of Problem According to LDDI	Children with Learning Disability		
	Attending Special Education (n=60)	Not Attending Special Education (n=60)	Total
Listening	58 (96.7)	54 (90.0)	112 (93.3)
Speaking	57 (95.0)	40 (66.7)	97 (80.8)
Reading	55 (91.7)	58 (96.7)	113 (94.2)
Writing	58 (96.7)	40 (66.7)	98 (81.66)
Mathematics	57 (95.0)	37 (61.7)	94 (78.3)
Reasoning	54 (90.0)	4 (6.7)	58 (48.33)

Table 4.7, shows the type of LD problems according to attending and not attending special education. Majority (94 per cent) of children had Reading problems followed by Listening (93 per cent), Writing (81.7 per cent), Speaking (80.8 per cent), Mathematics (78.3 per cent) and Reasoning (48.3 per cent) Problems.

General Information about LD Variables

Age of identification of LD is important to provide early intervention. Identification at earlier age helps providing appropriate remedial teaching. Usually the intervention includes special education classes, either in resource room or in full time special classes.

Among children identified with LD equal number of children (n=60) attending special education and not attending special education were included in the sample to enable comparison.

Table 4.8 shows the distribution of sample children with LD according to LD variables, like problem identified age, person who identified the problem and source of identification by significant others.

Table 4.8

Distribution of Sample Children with LD according to Variables related to LD (Percentages in Parenthesis)

S.No	Variables related to LD	Children with LD		Total
		Attending SE (n=60)	Not attending SE (n=60)	
1.	**Problem Identified age**			
	7 years	16 (26.7)	10 (16.7)	26 (21.7)
	8 years	32 (53.3)	39 (65.0)	71 (59.2)
	9 years	8 (13.3)	9 (15.0)	17 (14.2)
	10 years	4 (6.7)	2 (3.3)	6 (5.0)
2.	**Person who identified The Problem**			
	Teacher	47 (78.3)	59 (98.3)	106 (88.3)
	Parent	10 (16.7)	1 (1.7)	11 (9.2)
	Relatives/Others	1 (1.7)	0 (0.0)	1 (0.8)
	Doctors	2 (3.3)	0 (0.0)	2 (1.7)
3.	**Source of Identification by significant others**			
	Class work observation	48 (80.0)	51 (85.0)	99 (82.5)
	Based on marks	1 (1.7)	1 (1.7)	2 (1.7)
	Home work	11 (18.3)	8 (13.3)	19 (15.8)

The age group of sample was ranged between 8 years to 11 years. From the table 4.8, it is clear that among children with LD, majority (59.2 per cent) were identified as having problem at the age of 8 years. Next to it 21.7 per cent were identified at the age of 7 years, followed by 14.2 per cent of children at the age of 9 years and very few (5.0 per cent) children were identified with the problem of LD at the age of 10 years. The problems of LD will be identified mostly by teachers and parents generally by 8 years i.e. before the child reaches 4thstandard, as it is the age for learning basics of academic skills like reading, writing and mathematics. Early identification of problems in these aspects will be helpful for parents and teachers to take care and to provide special education.

Reported literature shows that early intervention with quality instruction improves outcomes for all students with learning failure including those with LD. It is more difficult to educate students with LD when they are older. Hence, age of identification plays a significant role not only to provide special education but also for better coping up by the children. Regina and Scholte (2012), reported that among the variables that are predictors for placement in special schools not only the academic performance but age at which child received special care for the first time is also important for placement in special schools.

Parents were asked to mention the person who identified that the child has problem related to LD.

From the table it is known that in 88.3 per cent of children with LD were identified as having problem by the class teachers. Teacher plays an important role in identifying the problems.

When parents and teachers were asked to mention the source from which they have identified theproblem as learning disability, it was reported that, majority of children were identified as having LD (82.5 per cent) based on class work observation. Next to it, children's home work helped in identification of problem (15.8 per cent). Very few (1.7 per cent) were identified as children with LD based on their marks, scored in examinations.

A study by National Institute of Health (2006), showed that 67 per cent of young students who were at risk for reading difficulties became average or above average readers after receiving help in the early grades. Early identification of LD will be helpful to provide early intervention and to improve their academic performance.

Problems Related to LD (As per Teachers' Perception)

Problems related to children with learning disability was collected from both teachers and mothers separately using check list for Problems Related to LD. Table 4.9 and 4.10 show the mean scores of the problems.

Table 4.9

Mean Scores of Problems Related to LD among Children (As per Teachers' Perception)

S.No.	Problems Related to LD	Mean Scores of Problems Related to LD				Total	
		Children Attending SE (n=60)		Children Not Attending SE (n=60)			
		Mean	SD	Mean	SD	Mean	SD
1.	Reading problems	10.95	2.819	14.25	1.284	12.60	2.739
2.	Writing Problems	11.32	2.759	12.23	2.258	11.78	2.552
3.	Mathematical Problems	10.53	2.587	12.52	2.771	11.53	2.849
4.	Syntax and LanguageProblems	10.77	2.560	9.02	1.157	9.89	2.165
5.	Visual PerceptualProblems	9.22	2.909	8.67	0.958	8.94	2.174
6.	Auditory perceptionProblems	8.72	2.394	8.98	1.000	8.85	1.832
7.	Visual receptionProblems	8.88	2.429	9.00	1.042	8.94	1.862
8.	Auditory receptionProblems	9.55	2.734	9.15	1.176	9.35	2.105
9.	Directional confusion	9.70	2.438	8.93	1.118	9.32	1.927
10.	Attention problems	10.57	2.375	9.48	1.467	10.03	2.039
11.	Problems in Academic Achievement	11.35	2.462	11.32	1.557	11.33	2.051
	Total	118.15	17.772	114.57	5.967	116.36	13.323

Table 4.9 shows mean scores of problems related to LD, as per teachers' perception. When the total mean score of children with LD irrespective of attending SE or not attending SE is considered from the table it is evident that teachers perceived reading problems as highest (mean=12.60; SD = 2.74) among sample children with LD. The mean scores were high for writing problems (mean =11.78; SD = 2.55) followed by problems in Mathematics (mean = 11.53; SD= 2.85) and problems in academic achievement (mean = 11.33; SD = 2.05). Comparatively the mean score were low in the areas of visual reception and visual and auditory perception problems (mean 8.94 and 8.85 respectively).

Generally teachers focus will be more on skills related to academic aspects like reading, writing and mathematics. The visual and auditory perception problems are mostly invisible and can be identified when parent or teacher have special knowledge in identifying the problem and may be the reason for low scores when compared to other problems.

Problems Related to LD (As per Parents' Perception)

Parenting children with learning disabilities presents special challenges, not only with the child's everyday problems, but also the associated social and emotional problems of school failure.

Table 4.10

Mean Scores of Problems Related to LD among Sample Children

S.No.	Relation to LD	Mean Scores of Problems Related to LD				Total	
		Children Attending SE (n=60)		Children Not Attending SE (n=60)			
		Mean	SD	Mean	SD	Mean	SD
1.	Reading problems	11.77	3.180	13.93	1.260	12.85	2.643
2.	Writing Problems	11.90	2.413	11.82	2.274	11.86	2.335
3.	Mathematical Problems	10.65	2.748	12.52	2.24	11.58	2.67
4.	Syntax and LanguageProblems	9.53	2.174	9.10	1.037	9.32	1.710
5.	Visual PerceptualProblems	8.63	1.97	8.85	0.685	8.74	1.47
6.	Auditory perceptionProblems	8.88	1.984	8.87	0.892	8.88	1.532
7.	Visual receptionProblems	9.10	1.829	8.83	0.994	8.97	1.472
8.	Auditory receptionProblems	9.73	2.024	8.83	0.924	9.28	1.631
9.	Directional confusion	9.43	2.273	8.62	1.059	9.03	1.812
10.	Attention	10.62	2.278	9.28	1.223	9.95	1.940
11.	Academic Achievement	13.22	2.344	11.87	1.282	12.54	2.000
	Total	113.08	12.586	112.40	4.319	112.74	9.376

Table 4.10 shows the mean scores of problems related to LD. Mothers' perceived reading problems as highest (Mean= 12.85; SD=2.643) followed by problems in academic achievement (mean=12.54; SD = 2.00) and writing problems (mean = 11.86; SD = 2.335). Mothers' identified least problems in Visual perceptual and auditory perceptual problems, may be due to the same reasons mentioned earlier for teachers.

Chapman and James (1999) in a study reported that mothers of LD Subjects showed more negative and fewer positive reactions to their children. They also held lower academic performance expectations for their children than control mothers.

Thus, from tables 4.9 and 4.10, it is evident that teachers and parents perceived more problems in areas of reading, writing and academic achievement, which are visible and can identified easily. As identification of other problems like Visual perception and auditory perceptual problems require more expertise and observation, creating awareness and education in these aspects will be helpful for parents to understand the problems related to LD of their children.

Problems related to LD scale was given to both parents and teachers. Correlation was calculated for the scores given by parents and teachers, and is presented below.

Correlation between Parents' and Teachers' Perception of Problems Related to LD

Karl Pearson's coefficient of correlation was computed to see the agreement between teachers and parents perception of problems related to LD.

Table 4.11 shows the correlation values.

Table 4.11

Correlation between Parents and Teacher Perception of Problems Related to LD

Variables	Problem Related to LD		Coefficient of Correlation	
	Mean	Std. Deviation	N	r-value
Total score as given by teachers	116.36	13.323	120	0.15
Total score as given by parents	112.74	9.376	120	P<0.05

Table 4.11 shows the mean, SD's and correlation between parent and teachers perception of problems related to LD.

The Karl Pearson's coefficient of correlation (r-value) was 0.15 which was significant at 0.05 level. Since significant correlation was found between the scores as given parents and teachers, for further analysis, the problem related to LD as given by teachers was considered to minimize repetition. These findings were inline with that of Greene (1996), who also reported that there was correlation in the various kinds of problem behaviours rated by teachers and parents and they were also inter correlated.

Coping up of Problems by Children with LD

The coping up of problems by children with LD was assessed using Checklist for Assessment of Coping up of Problems of Learning Disability. Higher the score indicates more coping up capacity by the child and vice versa.

Table 4.12 shows the distribution of sample children according to coping up of problem as given by the child.

From table 4.12 and fig 4.33, it is evident that on the whole the sample children felt that they have moderate coping up capacity with regard to problems related to LD. The minimum total score as per the check list was 51 and maximum was 153. The mean score of the total sample was found to be 116.83 (SD = 19.18), which shows that the sample had moderate coping up capacity of problems in different areas like home, school, emotional and social.

When coping up of problems between children attending SE and those not attending SE was observed, comparatively children attending SE class have more score in all areas viz., home, emotional, social than those who were not attending SE class which means as per the rationale of the scale children attending SE classes have more coping up capacity.

Table 4.12

Mean scores of coping up of problems related to LD in Different Areas (As given by children)

S.No.	Areas of Coping	Mean Scores of Coping up of Problem				Total	
		Children Attending SE (n=60)		Children Not Attending SE (n=60)			
		Mean	SD	Mean	SD	Mean	SD
1.	Home	32.62	5.533	26.37	3.464	29.49	5.565
2.	School/Educational	32.37	5.511	26.92	2.824	29.64	5.148
3.	Emotional	30.52	5.385	26.33	3.592	28.43	5.019
4.	Social	32.30	5.366	26.27	3.888	29.28	5.563
	Total	127.80	20.120	105.85	9.613	116.83	19.183

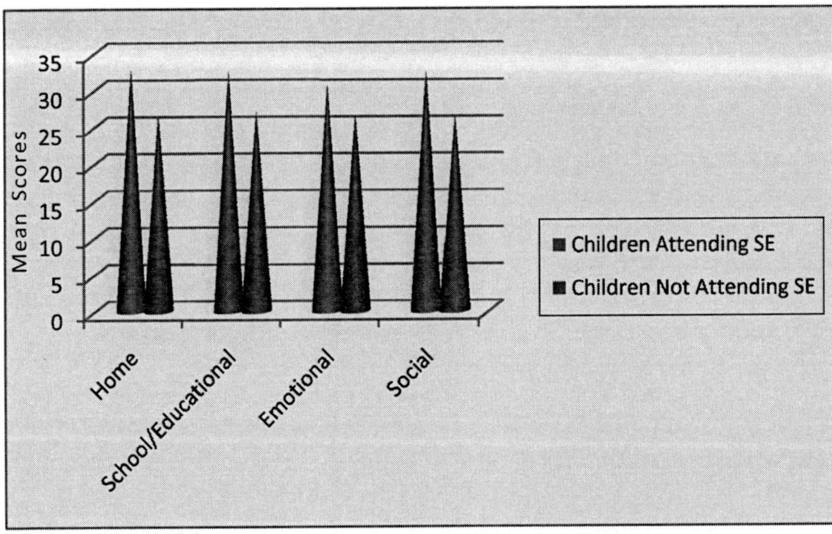

Fig. 4.3: Coping up of Problems Related to LD in Different Areas

Madhuri *et al,.*(2001) also reported that individualized remedial education plan, helps most children learn to cope up with disability and may get integrated in a regular stream.

Children who were not attending SE classes must be included in some type of SE to improve their coping up of problems and to make better adjustments.

Special Education Variables (n=60)

An array of special education services exists at International and in big cities at National level, where children with a variety of learning disabilities and different education plans can be placed in a program that works for them.

General Information about SE Variables

Special schools provide individualized education, addressing specific needs. Student-teacher ratios are kept low, often 6:1 or lower depending upon the needs of the children. Special schools will also have other facilities for the development of children with special needs, such as soft play areas, sensory rooms, or swimming pools, which are vital for the therapy of certain conditions. Full- Time Special Education provides individualized education, addressing specific needs.

Resource roomsare a part of normal schools where a special education program can be delivered to a student with a disability by a special educator.

Table 4.13 shows the distribution of sample according to SE variables.

Table 4.13

Distribution of Sample According to SE Variables (Percentages in Parenthesis)

S.No.	Special Education Variables	Children with LD Attending SE (n=60)
1.	**Person suggested special education**	
	Psychologist	4 (6.7)
	Teacher	54 (90.0)
	Relatives/Others	2 (3.3)
2.	**Type of special education**	
	Resource Room	16 (26.7)
	Full time SE	44 (73.3)
3.	**Duration of attending SE**	
	Below 6 months	10 (16.7)
	6 months – 1 year	36 (60.0)
	1 year – 2 years	14 (23.3)
4.	**Time spends in SE per day**	
	1 hour	16 (26.6)
	2 hours	14 (23.3)
	3 hours	30 (50.0)

The full time special education schools are available only at Hyderabad (in united Andhra Pradesh). In the other Districts (Nellore and Chittoor) where the samples were identified, theresource rooms were available, in which a special education teacher will be available for few hours per week.

From table 4.13 it is evident that among the samples who were identified as attending special education classes three fourths of sample (73.3 per cent) were attending full time special education. Nearly one fourth (26.7 per cent) were attending special education classes in resource room attached to the general school setup. Ninety per cent of sample children who were attending special education classes were attending the special classes based on the suggestion from the class teacher. Very few were referred by the psychologist and others (6.7 per cent and 3.3 per cent respectively).

Majority of sample children (60 per cent) were attending the special education classes from 6months to one year period. 16.7 per cent were attending for a period of below 6 months and 23.3 per cent for more than one year.

More than half of children attending SE were spending in SE classes 3 hours per day. Next to it 26.6 per cent were attending 1 hour per day in special education classes. Usually in resource room special classes will be provided for one hour only per day.

To see significant difference between children with and without LD in different areas of problems and adjustments t-test and Analysis of variance (ANOVA) were computed and presented in the following sections.

SECTION III

This section deals with the demographic variables and behaviour problems among children with and without LD. This section also includes relationship between demographic variables and parental perception of emotional reactions towards children's adjustments.

Demographic Variables and Behaviour Problems among Children with and without LD

Behaviour problems of children were assessed by teachers using Behaviour Problems Checklist (Anuradha and Bharathi, 2004). Teachers checked the behaviour problems exhibited by the children in four areas namely Home, Academic, Emotional and Social areas. Higher the score indicates more behaviour problems and vice versa.

Table 4.14 shows the mean scores of behaviour problems as perceived by the teachers among children with LD and without LD and f values.

Table 4.14

Mean Scores of Behaviour Problems Perceived by Teachers'

S. No.	Areas of Problems	Normal Achievers (Without LD)		Children with LD			
		Mean	SD	Mean	SD	t-value	sig
1.	Emotional	13.36	4.057	21.69	4.83	11.89	.000
2.	Home	12.71	4.036	22.17	5.67	15.47	.000
3.	Academic	13.39	4.458	22.90	4.59	14.71	.000
4.	Social	12.57	4.017	20.58	5.67	15.72	.000
	Total	52.04	13.780	87.31	16.26	21.21	.000

To assess whether children with and without LD differ in behaviour problems t-test was conducted. The t-values for all areas of problems viz, emotional, home, academic and social were highly significant which indicates that children with and without LD differed significantly in exhibiting behaviour problems. Comparatively teachers perceived more problems for children with LD than those without LD.

Reported studies on behaviour problems of children with LD and without LD have shown that comparatively children with LD have more behaviour problems than children without LD (Stephanie and David, 1986, Juvonen and George, 1992, Lardieri, Blaches and Swanson, 2000, James, 2002 and Michaels, 2004). Paul (1990), also reported that students of LD have more behaviour problems as per teacher's rating. Valence (2001) also reported that there were significant difference in social skills and problem behaviour between children with and without learning disability.

The failure in learning academic skills might be reflected in problem behaviour in other areas like social, emotional etc which might be perceived as problem behaviour by the teachers.

Child Variables and Behaviour Problems among Children with and without LD

To assess whether teacher's perception of behaviour problems varied according to child, parent and family variables.t-test and analysis of variance (ANOVA) were performed.The results are presented in table 4.15.

From the table 4.15 it is evident that as per teacher's perception among normal achievers, there was significant difference between boys and girls in the areas of emotional (t =3.21 and p< .002) and home (t =2.00 and p< .047) and total score (t =2.08 and p< .040). Comparatively teachers perceived more problems among girls in these areas than boys. When children with LD were considered, significant difference between boys and girls was observed in home area of adjustment (t =.044 and p< .034) and in total (t=0.06 and p< .050). There was no gender difference in other areas of adjustment like emotional, academic and social adjustments.

Table 4.15

Mean Scores of Behaviour Problems of Sample as Perceived by Teachers (SDs in Parenthesis) according to Child Variables

S.No.	Child Variables	Children without LD (Normal Achievers)					Children with LD				
		Emotional	Home	Academic	Social	Total	Emotional	Home	Academic	Social	Total
1	2	3	4	5	6	7	8	9	10	11	12
1.	Gender										
	Girls	14.33 (5.03)	13.33 (4.33)	13.81 (4.79)	12.74 (3.95)	54.20 (15.67)	22.6 (4.35)	23.56 (4.93)	23.35 (4.94)	21.49 (5.16)	91.05 (14.80)
	Boys	12.26 (2.04)	12.01 (3.56)	12.91 (4.02)	12.39 (4.10)	49.57 (10.83)	21.6 (5.01)	21.39 (5.93)	22.65 (4.39)	20.06 (5.90)	85.22 (16.75)
	t- Value	**3.21** P< 0.002**	**2.00* P<0.047**	**1.23@ P< 0.219**	**0.53@ P< 0.594**	**2.08* P< 0.040**	**0.104@ P< 0.091**	**0.044@ P< 0.034**	**0.426@ P< 0.442**	**0.188@ P< 0.172**	**0.060@ P< 0.0522**
2.	Age										
	8 years	12.98 (3.72)	12.86 (4.40)	13.14 (4.09)	12.53 (3.98)	51.51 (14.09)	22.37 (4.47)	23.54 (5.27)	23.54 (3.60)	21.83 (4.91)	91.29 (13.34)
	9 years	13.73 (4.56)	11.73 (3.36)	13.00 (4.45)	11.43 (1.82)	49.89 (11.01)	22.54 (4.70)	22.74 (5.04)	23.03 (4.31)	21.94 (5.52)	90.29 (15.44)
	10 years	12.72 (2.06)	12.67 (3.46)	13.26 (4.71)	12.69 (4.69)	51.33 (10.57)	20.46 (5.378)	21.18 (6.441)	22.18 (5.348)	19.32 (6.886)	83.21 (19.08)
	11 years	14.26 (5.40)	13.74 (4.78)	14.39 (4.69)	13.84 (4.79)	56.23 (18.79)	20.82 (4.66)	20.32 (5.84)	22.59 (5.48)	18.00 (4.22)	81.45 (16.01)
	f - Value	**1.064@ P <0.367**	**1.437@ P<0.234**	**0.664@ P<0.576**	**2.007@ P<0.106**	**1.317@ P<0.271**	**1.455@ P<0.231**	**1.912@ P<0.131**	**0.495@ P<0.687**	**3.416@ P<0.020**	**2.747@ P<0.046**

(Table Contd...)

1	2	3	4	5	6	7	8	9	10	11	12
3.	**Birth order**										
	1st born	13.21 (4.18)	12.08 (3.47)	12.64 (3.64)	11.95 (3.07)	49.89 (11.78)	21.[illegible] (4.2[illegible])	23.71 (4.20)	22.18 (4.08)	22.75 (4.94)	90.25 (13.38)
	2nd born & above	13.46 (3.98)	13.15 (4.34)	13.91 (4.89)	13.00 (4.52)	53.52 (14.88)	21.7[illegible] (5.2[illegible])	21.03 (6.34)	23.43 (4.89)	18.97 (5.66)	85.13 (17.87)
	t Value	**0.057@ P<0.811**	**7.053** P<0.009**	**6.697* P<0.011**	**8.011** P<0.005**	**4.681@ P< 0.032**	**5.2[illegible]* P<0.[illegible]24**	**6.421* P<0.013**	**2.635@ P<0.107**	**1.096@ P<0.297**	**3.784* P<0.054**
4.	**Grade**										
	3rd class	13.30 (4.33)	12.67 (4.09)	12.58 (3.35)	11.81 (2.81)	49.98 (11.39)	22.[illegible]5 (4.[illegible])	22.77 (5.94)	23.09 (4.09)	20.79 (5.45)	89.11 (15.96)
	4th class	12.92 (2.99)	11.14 (2.68)	13.35 (4.18)	11.51 (1.47)	49.12 (7.98)	21.[illegible] (4.7[illegible])	21.50 (5.66)	22.90 (5.16)	20.34 (6.12)	85.78 (16.62)
	5th class	14.02 (4.66)	14.33 (4.51)	14.20 (5.46)	14.35 (5.79)	56.90 (18.22)	21.[illegible]7 (4.[illegible])	22.39 (5.176)	22.52 (4.40)	20.65 (5.28)	86.96 (16.40)
	f- Value	**1.053@ P<0.351**	**8.84* P<0.000**	**1.635@ P<0.199**	**3.413* P<0.000**	**5.127** P<0.007**	**1.0[illegible]@ P<0.[illegible]57**	**0.622@ P<0.539**	**0.114@ P<0.892**	**0.077@ P<0.926**	**0.509@ P<0.602**
5.	**IQ**										
	Below average	13.30 (4.131)	12.48 (4.182)	14.52 (5.740)	12.19 (3.823)	52.11 (16.06)	21.[illegible]4 (5.[illegible]8)	17.68 (5.361)	23.57 (4.670)	17.50 (5.433)	79.96 (15.557)
	Average	13.75 (4.591)	13.05 (4.287)	13.42 (3.820)	13.01 (4.259)	53.34 (14.20)	21.[illegible]0 (4.[illegible]7)	23.39 (5.082)	22.77 (4.455)	21.32 (5.384)	89.22 (16.002)
	Above average	12.37 (4.29)	11.87 (2.921)	12.13 (2.432)	11.57 (3.234)	47.93 (8.998)	22.[illegible]1 (4.7[illegible]9)	24.11 (4.993)	22.39 (5.169)	22.28 (5.696)	90.89 (15.770)
	f- value	**1.105@ P<0.334**	**1.036@ P<0.357**	**2.533@ P<0.083**	**1.633@ P<0.199**	**1.767@ P<0.174**	**0.2[illegible]3@ P<0.[illegible]69**	**14.090* P<0.000**	**0.436@ P<0.648**	**6.053** P<0.003**	**3.993* P<0.021**

@ Not significant

* 0.01 level

** 0.05 level (Same notation are followed throughout the report)

Gethanjali (2004) in an Indian study also reported that LD child had more problems in social and emotional adjustments and there was significant gender effectsamong children with LD. But in present, study there was no significant difference in the problem between boys and girls among children with and without LD. However, these findings are in line with that of Margaret and Margaret (2010). They also found that regardless of disability status girls reported more emotion systems index, social stress and depression.

When behaviour problems were considered age wise, there was no significant difference observed among normal achieving children. But among children with LD significant difference in behaviour problems score were observed in social area (f=3.41 and p< .020) and total score (f=2.74 and p< .046). Among children with LD it was observed that with the increase in age, the intensity of behaviour problems decreased significantly in social area and also in overall problems. Baum *et al.,* (1998),that in a study on social dysfunctionobserved, children with LD reported the need for social skills intervention to improve social adjustment. In the present study special education received by children with LD might have helped the students to improve social adjustments, hence the score for behaviour problemsdecreased.

As per birth order the normal achievers differed significantly in all areas except in emotional area. Among children with learning disability the sample children significantly differed in the areas Viz., emotional, home and total score according to their order of birth. From the table it is known that comparatively the mean scores of behaviour problems for first born children were more than later born. Akhil and Tushar (2013), in their study on prevalence and pattern of learning disabilities in school children also reported that with the increases in number of siblings, there is decrease in number of positive cases of learning disabilities.

When children without LD were compared against grade, significant difference was found in the areas of home (f=8.84 and p<.000), social (f =8.41 and p<.000) and total adjustment (f=5.13 and p<.007). No significant difference was found among children with learning disability in all areas of behaviour problems according to the children's grade. However, when compared with children without LD the means scores in all areas were higher for children with LD.

As per Intelligence Quotient (IQ), it can be interpreted from table 4.16 that the mean scores of problems in academic area have decreased with increase of IQ for both the groups of children that is those with LD and without LD. However, the difference is significant among children without LD (f = 2.53: P<0.83). Children with LD significantly differed in the area of home (f=14.08; p<0.00), social (f=6.53; p<.003) and total (f=3.99; p<.021) according to their IQ.In these three areas (home, social and total), the intensity of behaviour problems were more for children with above average Intelligence than those who had below average IQ as per teachers' perception.

If children had more IQ and had the problems of LD, the inability to satisfy parents at home and compete with peers might have made children to exhibit more behaviour problems. Miglani *et al.*, (2011), in a study on the intelligence and achievement motivation among learning disabled children and non-learning disabled children used RSPM (Raven's Successive Progressive Matrices) to measure intelligence and GLAD (Grade Level Assessment Device, 1997) to measure need for motivation. No significant difference was observed in intelligence, but children without learning disabilities showed higher need for motivation than children with learning disabilities.

Demographic Variables and Parental Perception of Emotional Reactionstowards Children's Adjustments

Table 4.16

Mean Scores of Parental Perception of Emotional Reactions towards Children's Adjustments

Areas of Children's Adjustments	Children without LD (Normal Achievers)		Children with LD		t-value	Sig
	Mean	SD	Mean	SD		
Academic	30.17	7.675	27.42	7.83	8.98	0.000
Home	30.37	6.308	26.24	8.40	10.25	0.000
Emotional	29.89	6.539	24.44	8.06	20.67	0.000
Social	28.41	5.815	20.29	6.91	57.11	0.000
Total	118.60	23.175	97.38	26.15	30.33	0.000

Table 4.16 shows the mean scores of parental perception of emotional reactions towards children adjustments with and without LD and t-values. It divulges from table that children with LD differed significantly from children without LD in all areas of adjustment as per parent's perception. Comparatively parents of children with LD perceived more stress than those of without LD.

These findings were in line with the studies of Dyson (2006) and Doleys *et al.*, (1976), who found that mothers of LD children think that their children had more behavioural and adjustment problems.

Comparatively mothers perceived less stress in academic area of adjustments may be due to lower academic performance expectations for their children. Chapman (1999), also reported that mothers of LD children held lower academic performance expectations of their children than normally achieving children (controlled mothers).

Child Variables and Parents' Perception of Children's Adjustments

The third objective of the study was "To assess the relationship among child, parent and family variables with parent's Perception of Emotional Reactions towards Children's adjustments. t/f test and analysis of variance were performed.

Table 4.17 shows mean scores of Perception of Emotional Reactions towards Children's adjustments, according child variables.

From the table 4.17 it is evident that as per parent's perception, no significant gender difference was found between children without LD and with LDin all areas of adjustments.

A perusal of table 4.17 shows that though, the differences were not significant comparatively parents of children with LD perceived more stress in all areas of adjustments than parents of children without LD.

Chandramukhi *et al.*,(2012), reported that there is a need to educate parents to lower their expectations for children with LD. Lurae and Johnson (2008), also reported that overall low average performance of a child was a better predictor for problem behaviour at school than having a specific learning disability.

When adjustment problems were considered age wise, there was significant difference observed in children without LD in the areas of academic (f = 6.026 and p<.001), home (f = 5.23 and p<.002), emotional (f=5.26 and p<.002), social (3.71 and p<.013) and total score (f=5.69 and p<.001). Whereas, children with LD differed significantly in the areas of academic (f 3.708 and p< .013) and social (f=5.26 and p<.002). As the age increased parents of normal achieving children perceived less stress in all areas of adjustments and parents of children with LD expressed more stress.

As per birth order, no significant difference was observed in all areas of adjustment among children without LD and with LD.When mean scores were observed no much difference was observed for normal achievers.But parental perception of stress was comparatively low for later born than first born children.

Akhil and Tushar (2013), in their study on prevalence and pattern of learning disabilities in school children also reported that with the increases in number of siblings, there is decrease in number of positive cases of learning disabilities.

When children without LD were compared against grade, significant difference was found in the areas of academic (f=6.65 and p<.002), home (f 3.20 and p< .042), emotional (f 6.53 and p< .002) and total score (f 5.69 and p < .004). No significant difference was found among children with learning disability except in one area i.e. social (f=3.37 and p<.038) according to the children's grade.

Table 4.17

Mean Scores of Perception of Emotional Reactions towards Children's Adjustments, according Child Variables

(SDs in parenthesis)

S.No.	Child Variables	Normal Achievers					Children with LD				
		Academic	Home	Emotional	Social	Total	Academic	Home	Emotional	Social	Total
1	2	3	4	5	6	7	8	9	10	11	12
1.	Gender										
	Girls	30.39 (7.342)	30.29 (6.076)	29.51 (6.555)	27.86 (5.322)	118.13 (22.282)	27.88 (7.672)	28.09 (8.326)	24.72 (7.845)	21.21 (6.682)	101.16 (24.989)
	Boys	29.93 (8.085)	30.46 (6.606)	30.31 (6.542)	29.03 (6.313)	119.14 (24.305)	27.17 ([illegible].954)	25.21 (8.444)	24.29 (8.225)	19.78 (7.029)	95.27 (26.716)
	t -Value	**0.133@ P<0.716**	**0.027@ P<0.870**	**0.560@ P<0.456**	**1.506@ P<0.222**	**0.072@ P<0.789**	**0.229@ P<0.634**	**3.254* P<0.074**	**0.080@ P<0.778**	**1.183 @P<0.279**	**1.404@ P<0.238**
2.	Age										
	8 years	27.37 (7.300)	27.98 (5.958)	27.12 (5.413)	26.86 (5.600)	109.65 (21.404)	25.23 (7.284)	25.83 (8.497)	22.46 (6.577)	17.00 (6.638)	90.86 (23.909)
	9 years	28.38 (7.959)	29.73 (6.017)	29.32 (6.791)	27.16 (4.494)	114.30 (22.055)	28.31 (8.700)	26.06 (8.189)	25.89 (8.341)	22.60 (5.430)	102.80 (26.575)
	10 years	33.21 (5.930)	31.18 (6.021)	31.95 (6.840)	30.44 (6.431)	125.79 (22.210)	26.61 (7.544)	25.75 (9.423)	24.82 (8.932)	22.18 (6.183)	96.61 (26.592)
	11 years	32.39 (8.073)	33.42 (6.276)	31.81 (6.002)	29.48 (5.960)	127.10 (23.194)	30.55 (6.731)	27.82 (8.045)	24.82 (8.517)	19.45 (8.376)	100.14 (27.761)
	f -Value	**6.026** P<0.001**	**5.229** P<0.002**	**5.264** P<0.002**	**3.708** P<0.013**	**5.697** P<0.001**	**[illegible].419** P<0.070**	**0.312** P<0.816**	**1.122@ P<0.343**	**5.259** P<0.002**	**1.327@ P<0.269**

(Table Contd...)

1	2	3	4	5	6	7	8	9	10	11	12
3.	**Birth Order**										
	1st born	29.61 (7.747)	30.64 (7.071)	29.95 (6.579)	28.49 (6.212)	118.92 (24.962)	26.75 (9.340)	25.80 (9.191)	23.90 (7.653)	19.82 (7.011)	95.10 (28.199)
	2nd born and above	30.56 (7.645)	30.18 (5.761)	29.84 (6.549)	28.35 (5.562)	118.38 (22.009)	27.93 (6.522)	26.57 (7.970)	24.84 (8.382)	20.64 (6.871)	99.07 (24.616)
	f Value	**0.559@ P<0.456**	**0.191@ P<0.663**	**0.010@ P<0.921**	**0.022@ P<0.883**	**0.019@ P<0.890**	**0.667@ P<0.416**	**0.235@ P<0.629**	**0.396@ P<0.531**	**0.405@ P<0.526**	**0.675@ P<0.413**
4.	**Grade**										
	3rd class	28.26 (7.682)	29.00 (6.382)	27.74 (5.576)	27.32 (5.751)	112.22 (21.984)	27.47 (7.961)	26.96 (8.493)	23.68 (6.975)	18.38 (6.582)	96.55 (25.322)
	4th class	29.00 (7.279)	30.00 (6.024)	29.64 (6.568)	27.96 (4.949)	116.60 (21.813)	26.90 (7.541)	26.16 (9.065)	25.30 (8.993)	21.94 (6.082)	98.66 (27.442)
	5th class	33.26 (7.230)	32.10 (6.234)	32.28 (6.722)	29.94 (6.438)	126.98 (23.596)	28.48 (8.404)	24.96 (7.239)	24.13 (8.159)	20.61 (8.452)	96.30 (26.015)
	f Value	**6.650** P<0.002**	**3.240** P<0.042**	**6.530** P<0.002**	**2.827** P<0.062**	**5.686** P<0.004**	**0.318@ P<0.729**	**0.430@ P<0.652**	**0.506@ P<0.604**	**3.366** P<0.038**	**0.101@ P<0.904**
5	**IQ**										
	Below average	34.78 (5.944)	33.67 (4.385)	32.22 (3.876)	29.67 (5.152)	130.44 (13.888)	28.79 (3.247)	26.75 (7.326)	23.11 (7.083)	21.50 (7.026)	98.25 (20.508)
	Average	28.31 (7.870)	29.42 (6.657)	29.40 (7.347)	28.31 (6.364)	115.12 (25.928)	26.14 (8.377)	25.50 (8.584)	24.19 (8.653)	19.39 (6.985)	94.32 (27.719)
	Above average	31.80 (6.397)	30.33 (5.797)	29.30 (5.364)	27.57 (4.384)	118.73 (16.860)	30.61 (9.488)	28.50 (9.679)	27.56 (6.336)	22.11 (6.096)	108.61 (25.435)
	f value	**9.175* P<0.000**	**4.998** P<0.008**	**2.135@ P<0.122**	**0.959@ P<0.386**	**.4.811** P<0.009**	**3.016* P<0.053**	**0.971@ P<0.382**	**1.787@ P<0.172**	**1.698@ P<0.188**	**2.224@ P<0.113**

As per Intelligence Quotient, among children without LD significant difference was observed in the areas of academic (f=9.17 and p<.000), home (f=4.99 and p<.008) and over all adjustment (f=4.81 andp<.009). Whereas, children with LD were significantly differed in the academic area only (f=3.02 and p<.053) according to their IQ. The data in table 4.18 reveals that irrespective of problems of LD, parents perceived less stress for those children who had above average intelligence.

Parent Variables and Parents' Perception of Emotional Reactions towards Children's Adjustments

Table 4.18 shows mean scores of parental perception of emotional reactions towards children's adjustments according to father's education and occupation.

From the table 4.18 it is clear that when father's education was considered significant difference was not observed among children with LD. Whereas parents perception towards children's adjustment with regard to children without LD differed significantly in the areas of academic (f 3.63 and p< .029), home (f =2.97 and p< .054) and total score of adjustment (f= 62.78 and p<.065). Comparatively parents with higher educational qualification perceived more problems than those with lower education qualification. Parents with higher educational qualification are more concerned about their children's academic achievement and might be more worried and might have perceived more problems than the parents with lower educational qualification.

When father's occupation was considered parents of childrenwithout LD differed significantly in their perception of children's adjustment problems in areas viz., academic (f=6.02 and p<.001), home (f=3.22 and p<.025) and total score of adjustment (f=2.84 and p<.040). Comparatively children of Govt/Private employees and those from families where father's occupation was agriculture seemed to have perceived more problems than those parents whose occupations were business and daily labour work.

Table 4.19 shows mean scores of parental perception of emotional reactions towards children's adjustments according to mother's education and occupation.

From the table 4.19 it is clear that, there was no significant difference in parent's perception of children's adjustment in all areas of adjustments among two groups of children that is children with and without LD according to mother's education.

When mother's occupation was considered significant difference was found in mother's perception of emotional reactions towards children's adjustment in all areas for children without LD. But there was no significant difference in all areas of adjustments among children with LD according to mother's occupation.

Table 4.18

Mean Scores of Parental Perception of Emotional Reactions towards Children's Adjustments According to Father's Education and Occupation

S.No.	Parental Variable	Adjustment Problems									
		Children without LD (Normal Achievers)					Children with LD				
		Academic	Home	Emotional	Social	Total	Academic	Home	Emotional	Social	Total
1.	**Fathers' Education**										
	Illiterate	31.86 (6.50)	30.10 (5.75)	29.17 (5.41)	27.66 (4.43)	118.52 (17.11)	26.59 (6.92)	24.98 (8.51)	23.34 (8.11)	20.75 (7.042)	94.16 (25.256)
	Up to 10th	30.94 (7.562)	31.43 (5.422)	30.91 (5.473)	28.89 (4.385)	122.20 (18.466)	28.08 (7.211)	26.84 (7.482)	25.04 (8.379)	19.40 (6.331)	99.00 (25.894)
	Intermediate and above	27.57 (8.145)	28.55 (7.772)	28.45 (8.597)	28.02 (8.478)	111.88 (32.120)	27.82 (8.872)	27.04 (8.926)	25.10 (7.918)	20.33 (7.160)	99.37 (27.270)
	f value	**3.630** P<0.029**	**2.971** P<0.054**	**2.188@ P<0.116**	**0.598@ P<0.551**	**2.785** P<0.065**	**0.399@ P<0.672**	**0.774@ P<0.464**	**0.644@ P<0.527**	**0.302@ P<0.740**	**0.525@ P<0.593**
2.	**Fathers' Occupation**										
	Daily Labour	31.80 (6.397)	30.33 (5.797)	29.30 (5.364)	27.57 (4.384)	118.73 (16.860)	28.83 (3.256)	26.70 (7.055)	23.43 (7.347)	21.78 (6.948)	97.35 (19.699)
	Govt/private employee	34.06 (6.800)	33.00 (4.822)	31.88 (4.540)	28.76 (5.339)	127.79 (16.490)	25.33 (8.771)	24.63 (9.394)	24.11 (8.626)	20.15 (6.701)	94.70 (29.311)
	Business	28.56 (7.172)	29.98 (5.321)	30.16 (5.734)	28.82 (3.570)	116.98 (18.231)	27.19 (8.324)	26.04 (9.058)	24.27 (8.521)	18.27 (6.558)	94.96 (28.199)
	Agriculture/others	27.41 (8.739)	28.34 (8.638)	27.91 (9.556)	28.13 (9.577)	111.78 (36.239)	28.11 (8.551)	27.11 (8.367)	25.27 (7.978)	20.80 (7.174)	100.48 (26.372)
	f value	**6.015** P<0.001**	**3.22** P<0.025**	**2.162@ P<0.095**	**0.361@ P<0.781**	**2.844@ P<0.040**	**1.009@ P<0.391**	**0.501@ P<0.683**	**0.289@ P<0.833**	**1.186@ P<0.318**	**0.368@ P<0.776**

Table 4.19

Mean Scores of Parent Perception of Emotional Reactions towards Children's Adjustments according to Mother's Education and Occupation

S. No.	Parental Variable	Adjustment Problems									
		Children Without LD (Normal Achievers)					Children with LD				
		Academic	Home	Emotional	Social	Total	Academic	Home	Emotional	Social	Total
1.	**Mothers' Education**										
	Illiterate	32.00 (6.885)	30.00 (5.958)	29.81 (5.767)	28.43 (4.760)	119.86 (18.459)	[illegible]57 ([illegible]87)	26.32 (8.172)	24.14 (7.793)	21.25 (6.868)	97.84 (24.697)
	Up to 10th Class	30.43 (7.407)	30.81 (5.499)	30.22 (5.526)	28.23 (4.436)	119.42 (18.804)	[illegible].09 ([illegible]91)	25.04 (8.600)	24.65 (9.291)	19.26 (6.447)	95.52 (27.933)
	Intermediate and above	27.89 (8.862)	29.04 (8.867)	28.75 (9.823)	29.04 (9.819)	114.71 (37.181)	[illegible].45 ([illegible]318)	26.70 (8.789)	24.60 (7.863)	19.94 (7.169)	97.81 (27.009)
	f value	**1.908@ P<0.152**	**0.909@ P<0.405**	**0.551@ P<0.578**	**0.210@ P<0.811**	**0.484@ P<0.617**	**0[illegible]29@ P<[illegible].972**	**0.304@ P<0.738**	**0.049@ P<0.952**	**0.743@ P<0.478**	**0.071@ P<0.932**
2.	**Mothers' Occupation**										
	House wife	30.97 (7.204)	30.92 (5.406)	30.41 (5.354)	28.48 (4.310)	120.48 (17.811)	[illegible].03 ([illegible]522)	25.85 (8.577)	23.87 (8.024)	20.19 (6.890)	95.78 (26.022)
	Daily Labour	20.25 (.957)	21.25 (1.708)	20.00 (.816)	20.25 (1.500)	81.75 (4.193)	[illegible].19 ([illegible]555)	26.19 (8.216)	24.19 (9.138)	19.31 (5.873)	94.63 (27.568)
	Govt/private employee	27.36 (8.880)	28.55 (9.180)	28.55 (10.034)	29.09 (10.281)	113.55 (38.111)	[illegible].44 ([illegible]882)	25.94 (6.767)	23.75 (7.793)	19.06 (8.873)	93.94 (24.181)
	Bussines	29.50 (10.521)	30.50 (10.193)	30.00 (11.593)	30.00 (11.916)	120.00 (44.095)	[illegible]3.09 ([illegible].319)	27.27 (12.370)	26.36 (8.721)	21.09 (5.166)	101.91 (31.716)
	Agriculture/others	28.20 (8.892)	29.40 (8.784)	29.00 (9.752)	29.10 (9.315)	115.70 (36.609)	[illegible]3.56 ([illegible]784)	28.56 (6.425)	28.11 (6.133)	24.00 (6.801)	115.00 (17.037)
	f value	**2.647** P<0.036**	**2.723** P<0.032**	**2.765** P<0.030**	**2.230** P<0.069**	**3.060** P<0.019**	**[illegible]541@ P[illegible]0.169**	**0.243@ P<0.913**	**0.736@ P<0.569**	**0.891@ P<0.472**	**1.293@ P<0.277**

Family Variables and Parental Perception of Children's Adjustments

Table 4.20 shows the mean scores of parental perception of emotional reactions towards children's adjustments according to family variables.

Table 4.20

Mean Scores of Parental Perception of Emotional Reactions towards Children's Adjustments According to Family Variables

S.No.	Family Variables	Children without LD (Normal Achievers)						Children with LD			
		Academic	Home	Emotional	Social	Total	Academic	Home	Emotional	Social	Total
1.	Type of family										
	Nuclear	30.09 (7.391)	30.39 (6.208)	29.88 (6.567)	28.41 (5.953)	118.51 (22.956)	27.43 (7.921)	25.97 (8.402)	24.33 (7.856)	19.80 (6.969)	96.59 (25.85)
	Joint	30.93 (10.166)	30.20 (7.389)	29.93 (6.508)	28.33 (4.546)	119.40 (25.909)	27.36 (7.376)	28.29 (9.118)	25.29 (9.770)	24.00 (5.335)	103.36 (28.66)
	t Value	**0.162@ P<0.687**	**0.012@ P<0.915**	**0.001@ P<0.977**	**0.003@ P<0.959**	**0.020@ P<0.888**	**0.001@ P<0.973**	**0.920@ P<0.339**	**0.173@ P<0.679**	**4.703** P<0.032**	**0.825@ P<0.365**
2.	Income (Rs.)										
	Below 5000	33.33 (5.801)	30.17 (6.080)	30.78 (5.408)	29.06 (4.844)	122.89 (17.496)	29.44 (2.190)	27.56 (6.966)	24.75 (8.095)	22.69 (6.215)	101.44 (19.33)
	5000 to 10,000	30.19 (7.641)	30.69 (5.747)	30.01 (5.870)	28.16 (4.790)	118.79 (20.220)	29.45 (6.685)	28.55 (8.238)	25.57 (7.578)	20.77 (6.349)	103.83 (22.98)
	Above 10,000	27.84 (8.420)	29.12 (8.536)	28.72 (9.511)	29.00 (9.539)	114.68 (35.800)	25.19 (9.090)	23.96 (8.594)	23.42 (8.437)	19.23 (7.423)	90.93 (28.948)
	f Value	**2.744** P<0.068**	**0.636@ P<0.531**	**0.581@ P<0.561**	**0.581@ P<0.561**	**0.667@ P<0.515**	**4.685** P<0.011**	**4.209** P<0.017**	**0.932@ P<0.397**	**1.769@ P<0.175**	**3.495** P<0.034**

From table 4.20 it is known that children without LD did not differ significantly in the adjustment problems in all areas of adjustment according to their type of family. Children with LD differ significantly in the area of social adjustment (t=4.70 and p< .032) according to their type of family. Comparatively parents' perceived that children from joint families have good adjustments in academic area than those from nuclear families.

When family income was considered among children with and without LD significant difference was observed in academic area of adjustments according to their parents' perception for both the groups children with LD (f=2.74 and p<0.068) and without LD (f=4.69 and p<0.01). As the income range increased parents perceived more problems in academic area of adjustments.

SECTION IV

In this section relationship among LD variables and SE variables with behaviour problems and parental perception of emotional reactions towards children's adjustments is explained. This section also includes analysis of SE variables, problems related to LD and coping up of problems.

Relationship of LD and SE Variables, with Behaviour Problems and Parental Perception of Emotional Reaction towards Children's adjustments

The sample children with learning disability were 120. Among these sample, 60 students were those who were attending SE classes and 60 students were from normal schools who were not attending any special education classes.

LD Variables and Behaviour Problems

The LD variables of the study were type LD and duration of identification that the child is having learning disability.

Table 4.21 shows the mean scores of children's behaviour problems according to type of LD.

It divulges from table 4.21, that children did not differ significantly according to type of LD in all areas of behaviour problems except in the social area. The f-value for social area is 2.382 which was significant at 0.037 level.

A perusal of table 4.21 shows that children with LD had more behaviour problems in all areas viz., emotional, home, academic and social, irrespective of type of LD. Comparatively mean scores were more in academic area which shows that children had more problems in academic areathan in other areas. However, significant difference was observed in social area (f=2.38 : p< 0.037). The children had less problems in social area which showed good adjustments. If parents or teachers encourage social skills among children with LD they may excel in social functioning though, they were backward in academic area.

Table 4.21

Mean Scores of Behaviour Problems according to Type of LD and f-Values (SDs in Parenthesis)

S.No.	Type of LD	Areas of Behaviour Problems				
		Emotional	Home	Academic	Social	Total
1.	Listening	21.83 (4.91)	22.17 (5.66)	22.87 (4.69)	20.57 (5.61)	87.42 (16.21)
2.	Speaking	21.94 (4.96)	21.97 (5.87)	22.82 (4.74)	20.28 (5.79)	87.00 (16.57)
3.	Reading	21.51 (4.75)	22.27 (5.61)	22.78 (4.65)	20.58 (5.71)	87.12 (16.39)
4.	Writing	22.00 (5.08)	21.86 (5.97)	22.82 (4.794)	20.14 (5.86)	86.80 (17.13)
5.	Mathematics	21.95 (5.14)	22.12 (6.014)	23.00 (4.85)	19.96 (5.89)	87.01 (17.38)
6.	Reasoning	21.51 (5.51)	20.18 (6.394)	22.94 (5.07)	17.68 (5.48)	82.25 (17.70)
	f– Value	**0.178@ P<0.971**	**1.155@ P<0.330**	**0.027@ P<1.000**	**2.382** P<0.037**	**0.874@ P<0.498**

These findings are in line with Duncan and Matson (1999), who assessed the differences in social skills among severe and profound learning disabilities. The authors found that LD children's social behaviour differed depending on the level of disability.

The second LD variable is duration LD problem.

Table 4.22 shows the relationship between duration of LD and behaviour problems and f values

Table 4.22

Mean Scores of Behaviour Problems according duration of LD and f-values

S. No.	Duration of LD	Areas of Behaviour Problems				
		Emotional	Home	Academic	Social	Total
1.	6 months	22.05 (4.624)	22.32 (5.186)	23.41 (3.788)	20.45 (6.559)	88.23 (15.605)
2.	12 months	21.50 (4.758)	22.73 (5.682)	23.17 (4.158)	21.75 (5.869)	89.15 (16.752)
3.	24 months and above	21.72 (5.059)	21.56 (5.911)	22.42 (5.300)	19.50 (4.900)	85.14 (16.128)
	f – Value	**0.096@ P<0.908**	**0.526@ P<0.539**	**0.485@ P<0.617**	**1.967@ P<0.144**	**0.783@ P<0.459**

The results of analysis of variance showed that LD children did not differ significantly in all areas of behaviour problems depending on the duration of identification of LD. f-values were not significant. However, an observation of total scores of behaviour problems revealed that the intensity of behaviour problems decreased, when the duration of identification was more than 24 months and above period. As the duration of identification of learning disability among children increases, parents and teachers slowly understand the reasons for child's problem behaviour. Less pressure from parents and teachers may result in less problem behaviour among children.

Relationship of LD Variables with Parental Perception of Emotional Reactions towards Children's Adjustments

Table 4.23 shows the relationship between the emotional reactions of parents in different areas of adjustment according to type of LD.

Table 4.23

Mean Scores of Parental Perception of Emotional Reactions towards Children's Adjustments and f-values

S.No.	Type of LD	Areas of Parental Perception of Emotional Reactions Towards Children Adjustments				
		Academic	Homo	Emotional	Social	Total
1.	Listening	27.50 (7.60)	26.45 (8.46)	24.47 (8.13)	20.15 (6.84)	97.58 (25.74)
2.	Speaking	27.65 (7.48)	26.74 (8.54)	24.29 (8.17)	20.43 (6.81)	98.03 (26.02)
3.	Reading	27.45 (8.02)	26.41 (8.68)	24.58 (8.26)	20.23 (7.03)	97.71 (26.87)
4.	Writing	27.87 (7.32)	26.74 (8.60)	24.45 (8.29)	20.18 (6.75)	98.35 (25.84)
5.	Mathematics	27.92 (7.48)	26.81 (8.51)	24.70 (7.91)	20.35 (6.76)	98.88 (25.39)
6.	Reasoning	28.81 (6.08)	28.25 (8.05)	24.70 (7.68)	20.87 (6.51)	101.68 (22.90)
	f – Value	**0.312@ P<0.906**	**0.425@ P<0.831**	**0.033@ P<0.999**	**0.108@ P<0.990**	**0.239@ P<0.945**

When the total scores of problems related to LD according to parents' perceptionwas observed, it can be inferred that parents perceived more stress for those students who had listening and reading problems (mean=97.58 and mean=97.71 respectively). Next to it, speaking and writing problems (mean=98.03 and mean=98.35), followed by Mathematics and reasoning problems (mean=98.83 and mean=101.68). Comparatively the mean scores were more for those children who had reasoning problems, which shows that parents perceived less stress when the child has problems related to reasoning. However, the f-values were not significant for all areas of adjustments.

Table 4.24 shows the mean scores of parental perception of emotional reactions towards children adjustments according to duration of LD.

Table 4.24

Mean Scores of Parental Perception of Emotional Reactions towards Children Adjustments according to Duration of LD and f-values

S. No.	Duration of LD	Areas of Parental Perception of Emotional Reactions towards Children Adjustments				
		Academic	Home	Emotional	Social	Total
1.	6 months	25.86 (6.951)	28.50 (7.963)	23.82 (6.223)	18.36 (7.088)	96.91 (23.763)
2.	12 months	26.94 (8.509)	24.33 (7.929)	25.29 (9.072)	20.69 (7.282)	96.40 (27.908)
3.	24 months	28.58 (7.486)	27.08 (8.980)	23.90 (7.815)	20.76 (6.451)	98.54 (25.889)
	f - Value	**1.076[@] P<0.344**	**2.288[@] P<0.106**	**0.441[@] P<0.644**	**1.050[@] P<0.353**	**0.085[@] P<0.918**

From table 4.24, it is known that parental perception of emotional reactions towards children adjustments in different areas did not differ significantly according to duration of LD. The f-values were not significant.

The sample for the analysis included children with LD of two categories i.e., those attending special education and those not attending special education. Further analysis including special education in later tables will help to understand whether attending special education classes helps to decrease behaviour problems among children and also parental perception of stress towards children's adjustments.

Relation of SE Variables with Child's Problems, Adjustment and Coping up of Problems

SE Variables and Behaviour Problems

Special education or special needs education is the education of students with special needs in a way that addresses the students' individual differences and needs. Ideally, this process involves the individually planned and systematically monitored arrangement of teaching procedures, adapted equipment and materials, accessible settings, and other interventions designed to help learners with special needs to achieve a higher level of personal self-sufficiency and success in school and community than would be available, if the student were only given access to a typical classroom education.

Special education can be provided to children through resource rooms and full time classes. In the present study 60 children who were attending SE classes were included as sample for assessment of impact of SE.

SE variables of the study were type of SE, duration of SE and time spends in SE.

Table 4.25 shows the behaviour problems of children as given by teachers according to type of SE.

Table 4.25

Mean Scores of Behaviour Problems of Children (As per teachers' perception) according to Type of SE (SD's in parenthesis)

Type of SE	Mean Scores of Behaviour Problems				
	Emotional	Home	Academic	Social	Total
Resource Room	21.84 (6.061)	20.42 (6.355)	22.48 (5.644)	18.16 (5.657)	82.94 (20.434)
Full Time SE	20.83 (5.339)	19.41 (6.327)	23.00 (4.848)	16.07 (4.705)	79.10 (14.693)
t-value	0.468@ P<0.497	0.377@ P<0.542	0.143@ P<0.706	2.408@ P<0.126	0.687@ P<0.411

From table 4.25, it is known that children with LD who were attending resource room and full time SE did not differ significantly in their behaviour problems in all four areas of adjustment as per teacher's perception. The t-values were not significant. However, in all areas, comparatively children who were attending full time SE class have less problems than those who were attending resource room classes.

As the objective of both resource room and full time SE is providing extra academic skill training to children, no significant difference was observed in the adjustment problems according to type of SE classes children were attending. Nevertheless, in full time SE classes teachers spend more time with children and those teachers might have more understanding about children's problems than the teachers who teach for less time in resource room class.

Table 4.26 shows the relation between duration of attending SE and behaviour problems of children as per teacher's perception.

It divulges from table 4.26 that children with LD who were attending SE did not differ significantly in all areas of behaviour problemsi.e.emotional, home, academic and social areas depending on the duration of attending SE classes. The f-values were not significant. SE classes might have helped children to have less behaviour problems and the same can be interpreted from table 4.26. The magnitude of behaviour problems decreased as the duration of attending SE classes increased.

These finding are inline with that of Rogers and Saklofske (1985), who reported that LD children newly enrolled in resource room programs were significantly differed from LD children with more than six months of experience in such programs on the set of affective variables.

Table 4.26

Mean Scores of Behaviour Problems of Children according to duration of Attending SE

Duration of Attending SE	Mean Scores of Behaviour Problems				
	Emotional	Home	Academic	Social	Total
< 6 months	23.29 (5.345)	20.57 (3.309)	24.29 (3.592)	17.57 (6.949)	85.71 (13.099)
6-12 months	21.38 (5.865)	20.46 (7.211)	22.54 (5.637)	17.41 (5.524)	81.82 (19.720)
>12 months	20.29 (5.511)	18.14 (4.365)	22.50 (4.911)	16.21 (3.725)	76.71 (13.991)
f-Value	**0.641@ P<0.531**	**0.730@ P<0.486**	**0.341@ P<0.713**	**0.282@ P<0.755**	**0.681@ P<0.510**

Table 4.27 shows the duration of attending SE classes per day by children with LD and behaviour problems of children.

Table 4.27

Mean Scores of Behaviour Problems according to duration of Attending SE Classes

Time spends in SE Class	Mean Scores of Behaviour Problems				
	Emotional	Home	Academic	Social	Total
1 hour	24.67 (8.386)	22.67 (7.371)	25.33 (5.686)	21.33 (6.110)	94.00 (26.058)
2 hours	22.13 (6.462)	20.78 (6.494)	23.57 (4.934)	18.26 (5.754)	84.78 (20.340)
3 hours	20.53 (4.882)	19.12 (6.153)	21.94 (5.393)	16.03 (4.668)	77.44 (14.631)
f-Value	**1.079 P<0.347**	**0.768 P<0.469**	**1.051 P<.356**	**2.314 P<0.108**	**2.059 P<0.137**

From table 4.27, it is clear that, as the duration of time spent in SE classes increased the magnitude of behaviour problems in all areas of adjustments decreased. Comparatively, the teachers perceived less problems for the students who were attending SE for around 3 hours a day, than those for students who were attending less than 3 hours.

Attending SE classes helps students to understand their problems and will learn the techniques to cope up with the problems. Attending for more time in a SE class might have helped students to improve their adjustments in all areas of problem behaviour.

SE Variables and Parents' Perception of Emotional Reactions towards Children's Adjustments

Parents'perceptions of adjustment problems of children was assessed in four areas viz., academic, home, emotional and social areas.

Table 4.28 Shows mean scores of parents' perception of emotional reactions towards children's adjustments according to type of Special Education.

Table 4.28

Mean Scores of Parental Perception of Emotional Reactions towards Children's Adjustments according to Type of Special Education.

Type of SE	Mean Scores of Adjustment Problems				
	Academic	Home	Emotional	Social	Total
Resource Room	[illegible] (5.621)	[illegible] (6.824)	[illegible] (7.125)	21.86 (5.811)	107.45 ([illegible])
Full Time SE	29.45 (6.180)	27.48 (8.567)	25.13 (8.314)	20.90 (6.882)	101.00 (24.740)
t-value	**0.018@** **P<0.895**	**1.657@** **P<0.203**	**0.308@** **P<0.581**	**0.347@** **P<0.558**	**0.347@** **P<0.558**

From table 4.29, it is known that children with LD who were attending resource room and full time SE did not differ significantly in their adjustment problems in all four areas of adjustment as per parent's perception. The t-values were not significant. However, when the mean scores of adjustment problems were observed, parents perceived lessstress for children who were attending the full time SE classes when compared to those attending classes in resource rooms.

Parents who were more aware of their children's problems related to LD usually send their children to full time SE classes and the interaction between teachers and parents of children with LD will also be more while dropping and picking up of their children from special education classes. Based on the suggestions of teachers of SE classes, parents also help in practicing of different activities suggested by special teachers at home.

Table 4.29 shows the relation between duration of attending SE and parents' perception of emotional reactions towards children's adjustments.

It divulges from table 4.29, that children with LD who were attending SE differed significantly in academic and social areas (f=3.56:P<.035 and f=3.34: P<.042) depending on the duration of attending SE classes. The f-values were significant. Nevertheless, an insight into the table shows an encouraging trend in adjustment of children who were attending SE classes. In all areas of adjustments, the magnitude of problems decreased as the duration of attending SE classes increased.

Table 4.29

Mean Scores of Parents' Perception of Emotional Reactions towards Children's Adjustments according to Duration of Attending SE

Duration of Attending SE	Mean Scores of Adjustment Problems				
	Academic	Home	Emotional	Social	Total
< 6 months	25.43 (4.860)	30.43 (7.807)	23.57 (5.255)	18.71 (5.619)	98.14 (19.744)
6-12 months	29.31 (6.109)	27.82 (8.413)	25.08 (8.649)	20.59 (6.628)	101.77 (24.099)
>12 months	32.29 (4.340)	30.43 (5.932)	28.36 (5.257)	24.86 (4.055)	113.64 (14.627)
f-value	**3.568[@] P<0.035**	**0.753[@] P<0.475**	**1.232[@] P<0.299**	**3.346** P<0.042**	**1.819[@] P<0.171**

Rogers and saklofske (1985), also reported that LD children newly enrolled in resource room program were significantly differ from LD children with more than 6 months of experience in such programmes. It was reported that more experience helped in better adjustments.

Table 4.30 shows the relationship between parental perception of emotional reactions towards children's adjustments and time spent in Special Education classes per day.

Table 4.30

Mean Scores of Parental Perception of Emotional Reactions towards Children's Adjustments According to Time Spent in Special Education Classes per Day

Time spent in SE per day	Mean Scores of Adjustment Problems				
	Academic	Home	Emotional	Social	Total
1 hour	29.50 (5.669)	29.85 (6.942)	26.47 (7.166)	21.21 (5.629)	106.32 (18.729)
2 hours	27.33 (7.371)	25.67 (5.859)	21.67 (6.658)	21.00 (12.530)	99.00 (33.151)
3 hours	29.91 (6.193)	27.48 (9.145)	25.00 (8.660)	21.65 (6.582)	101.52 (25.895)
f-value	**0.253[@] P<0.777**	**0.872[@] P<0.424**	**0.666[@] P<0.518**	**0.039[@] P<0.962**	**0.399[@] P<0.673**

From table 4.30, it is clear that as the duration of time spent in SE classes increased, the adjustments in all areas seemed to be good. Comparatively as per parents perceptionscores were more for students who were attending SE for around 3 hours a day than those for students who were attending for 2 hours and 1 hour per day, which means better adjustments.

Attending SE classes for around 3 hrs per day helps students to understand their problems and techniques to cope up with the problems. Attending for more time in a SE class might have helped students to improve their adjustments.

SECTION V

This section consists of analysis of SE variables, problems related to LD and coping up of problems.

Learning disabilities are often present throughout the lifespan, so learning appropriate and effective methods of coping are essential to successful management of the disorder.

A diagnosis of a learning disability can be potentially devastating to an individual and their family. Both the individual and their family need to learn methods of coping with the effects of the disorder. Child also needs to learn how to cope with the disorder emotionally. Including teachers and parents as a part of the intervention will be helpful for children to cope up with problems successfully.

Analysis of SE Variables, Problems Related to LD and Coping up of Problems

The problems related LD are Reading, Writing, Mathematics, Syntax and Language Problems, Visual Perception, Auditory Perception, Visual reception, Auditory reception, Directional Confusion, Attention, Academic Achievement.

Problems related to LD scale was given to both parents and teachers. Correlation was calculated for the scores given by parents and teachers and as the correlation value was significant, the problems related LD given by teachers were considered for further analysis.

Mean Difference in Problems Related LD

Table 4.31 shows the mean difference in problems related to LD.

From the table 4.31 and fig. 4.4, it is clear that children with LD attending SE and not attending SE differed significantly in the areas of reading, mathematics, syntax and language and attention problems ($p<0.001$), followed by directional confusion and writing problems ($p<0.05$).

Table 4.31

Mean Difference in Problems Related to LD

Problems Related to LD	Children with LD				f-value	sig
	Attending SE (n=60)		Not attending SE (n=60)			
	Mean	SD	Mean	SD		
Reading problems	10.95	2.819	14.25	1.284	68.099	.000
Writing Problems	11.32	2.759	12.23	2.258	3.968	.049
Mathematical Problems	10.53	2.587	12.52	2.771	16.423	.000
Syntax and LanguageProblems	10.77	2.560	9.02	1.157	23.279	.000
Visual PerceptualProblems	9.22	2.909	8.67	0.958	1.935	.167
Auditory perceptionProblems	8.72	2.394	8.98	1.000	.634	.428
Visual receptionProblems	8.88	2.429	9.00	1.042	.117	.733
Auditory receptionProblems	9.55	2.734	9.15	1.176	1.084	.300
Directional confusion	9.70	2.438	8.93	1.118	4.904	.029
Attention Problems	10.57	2.375	9.48	1.467	9.037	.003
Problems Related to Academic Achievement	11.35	2.462	11.32	1.557	.008	.930

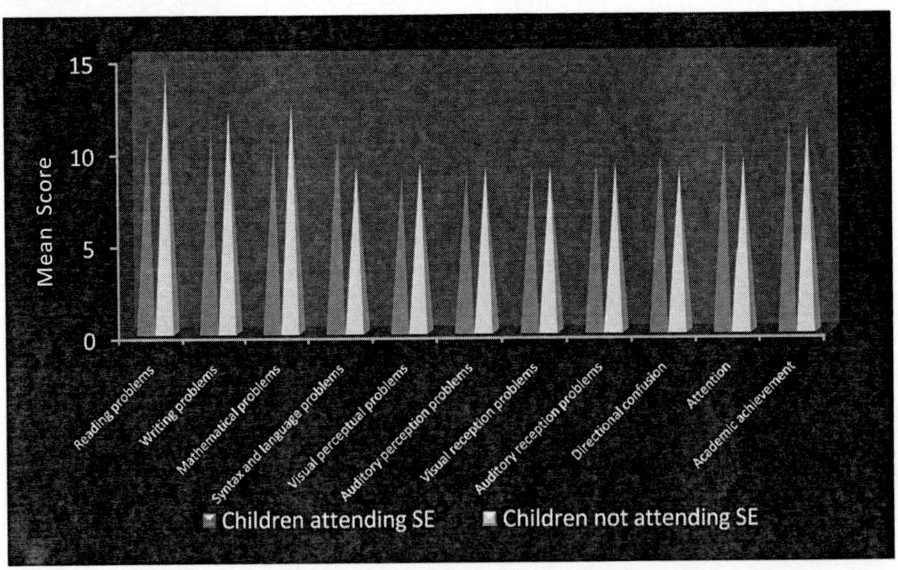

Fig. 4.4: Mean Scores of Problems Related to LD for Children Attending SE and not Attending SE

Table 4.32 shows the relation between problems related to LD and type of SE attended by the sample students.

Table 4.32

Mean Scores of Problems Related to LD according to Type of SE

Type of SE	Mean Scores of Problems related to LD											
	Reading	Writing	Mathematics	Syntax and Language Problems	Visual Perception	Auditory Perception	Visual Reception	Auditory Reception	Directional Confusion	Attention	Academic Achievement	Total
Resource room	13.21 (1.934)	13.10 (2.006)	11.86 (2.416)	11.41 (2.626)	9.28 (3.326)	8.86 (2.656)	8.90 (2.512)	10.14 (3.102)	11.38 (1.860)	10.55 (2.114)	13.07 (2.267)	120.17 (19.886)
Full time SE	8.84 (1.614)	9.65 (2.288)	9.29 (2.101)	10.16 (2.382)	8.10 (2.371)	8.58 (2.157)	8.87 (2.391)	9.00 (2.251)	8.13 (1.784)	10.58 (2.630)	9.74 (1.264)	116.26 (15.635)
f-value	**90.640** P<0.000**	**38.530** P<0.000**	**19.430** P<0.000**	**3.750* P<0.006**	**2.530@ P<0.120**	**0.204@ P<0.650**	**0.002@ P<0.971**	**2.670@ P<0.112**	**47.730* P<0.000**	**0.002@ P<0.963**	**50.150* P<0.000**	**0.723@ P<0.399**

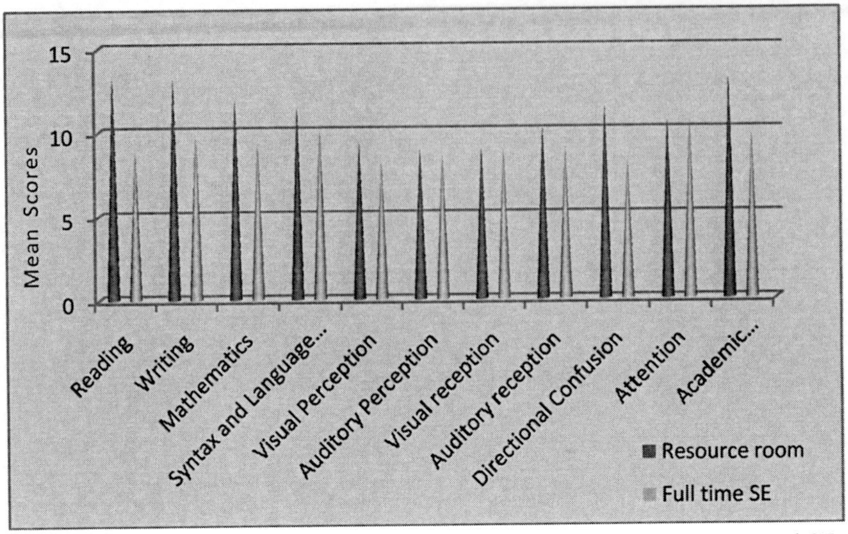

Fig. 4.5: Mean Scores of Problems Related to LD According to Type of SE

From the table 4.32 and fig. 4.5, it is known that there was significant difference between students who were attending special education classes in resource room and Full time SE in the problems viz., reading (t= 90.64), writing (t=38.53), Mathematics (t=19.43), directional confusion (t=47.73) and academic achievement (t=50.15). The t-values for these problems were significant at 0.01 level.

The SE teachers usually concentrate more for students who were attending full time SE classes on academics training than training in other types of problems. This might have helped students to have less degree of problems in reading, writing, mathematics, directional confusion and academic achievement areas.

Table 4.33 shows the relation between problems related to LD and duration of attending SE classes.

From the table 4.33 and fig. 4.6, it is evident that there was significant difference between students who were attending special education classes in resource room and full time classes in the problems viz., reading (f=7.88), writing (f=4.93), mathematics (f=7.34), syntax and language problems (f=10.14), visual perception problems (f=4.67) and academic achievement (f=24.08). The f-values for these problems were significant at 0.01 level. The magnitude of problems related LD were decreased when duration of SE classes increased. Students who were attending SE classes for more than 12 months were having less problems than those who were attending SE classes for 6-12 months and 6 months. Attending SE classes for longer period helps students to manage their problems better.

Table 4.33

Mean Scores of Problems Related to LD according to duration of Attending SE

Duration of SE	Mean Scores of Problems Related to LD											
	Reading	Writing	Mathematics	Syntax and Language Problems	Visual Perception	Auditory Perception	Visual Reception	Auditory Reception	Directional Confusion	Attention	Academic Achievement	Total
< 6 months	13.00 (2.51)	12.71 (2.49)	11.14 (1.952)	12.71 (1.976)	10.71 (3.450)	10.14 (.690)	10.14 (1.215)	10.57 (1.813)	10.00 (2.708)	11.00 (1.915)	12.43 (2.370)	129.00 (14.166)
6-12 months	11.36 (2.710)	11.72 (2.78)	11.18 (2.67)	11.21 (2.473)	8.30 (2.927)	8.67 (2.589)	8.87 (2.667)	9.56 (3.076)	10.10 (2.511)	10.56 (2.479)	12.23 (2.032)	117.95 (18.964)
>12 months	8.79 (1.968)	9.50 (1.99)	8.43 (1.22)	8.57 (1.505)	7.00 (1.569)	8.14 (2.179)	8.29 (2.016)	9.00 (1.961)	8.43 (1.697)	10.36 (2.405)	8.36 (0.497)	113.29 (14.166)
f-value	**7.88** P<0.001)**	**4.93** P<0.011**	**7.34** P<0.001**	**10.14* P<0.000**	**4.67** P<0.013**	**1.69@ P<0.193**	**1.38@ P<0.259**	**0.77@ P<0.469**	**2.63@ P<0.081**	**0.17@ P<0.847**	**24.08* P<0.000**	**1.89@ P<0.161**

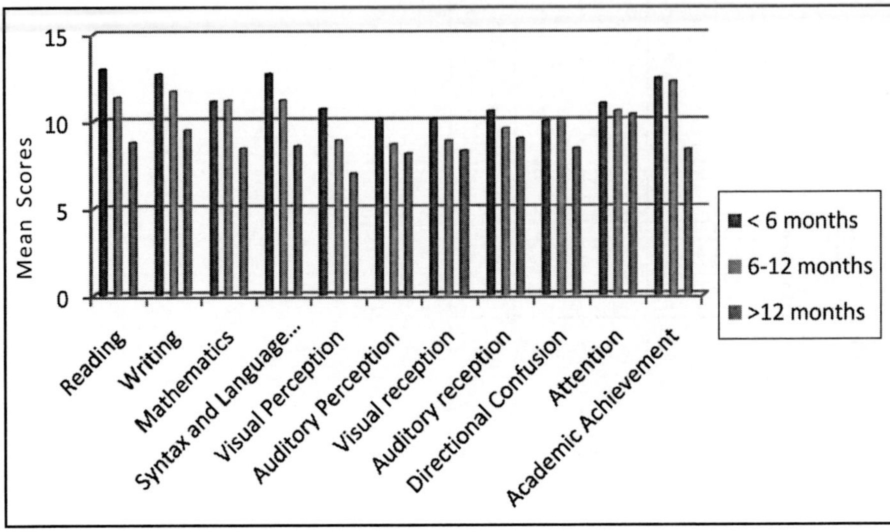

Fig. 4.6: Mean Scores of Problems Related to LD according to duration of Attending SE

Table 4.34 and fig. 4.7 indicate, that there was significant difference among students who were attending special education classes depending on the time spent in classes, in areas viz., reading (f= 45.13), writing (f=46.91), mathematics (f=5.94), directional confusion (f=11.79) and academic achievement (f=13.64). The f-values for these problems were significant at 0.01 level and for mathematic problems the f value was significant at 0.05 level. The SE classes were conducted for around 1 hour per day in resource room and for 1to 3 hours in full time SE classes.

In the table it is observed that the magnitude of problems were reduced when students have spent more time per day in SE classes. In one study Elaine and Lucian (1996), focused on academic, social, and behavioural adjustment for students declassified from Special Education. The authors analyzed data collected by the Michigan Department of Education and suggested that, as a group, students declassified from special education are academically, socially, and behaviourally well adjusted; but teachers or counselors of the declassified students felt that the students continued to require special education services. Within 3 years, the declassified students had returned to special education. Hence, education of teachers to accept children with LD is also important to reduce the problems related to LD.

Table 4.34 shows the relation between problems related to LD and time spent per day in SE classes.

Table 4.34

Mean Scores of Problems Related LD according to Time Spent in SE Classes per Day

Time spends in SE per day	Mean Scores of Problems Related to LD											
	Reading	Writing	Mathematics	Syntax and Language Problems	Visual Perception	Auditory Perception	Visual Reception	Auditory Reception	Directional Confusion	Attention	Academic Achievement	Total
1 hour	12.79 (2.171)	13.12 (2.027)	11.44 (2.414)	11.32 (2.495)	9.09 (3.059)	8.85 (2.560)	9.03 (2.406)	10.21 (2.911)	10.71 (2.195)	10.41 (2.258)	12.56 (2.312)	118.76 (19.638)
2 hours	11.00 (1.732)	11.67 (2.082)	10.33 (3.215)	9.67 (.577)	8.67 (4.041)	7.33 (1.528)	8.00 (1.732)	7.67 (3.055)	11.00 (2.646)	10.33 (1.528)	10.33 (3.215)	112.33 (17.926)
3 hours	8.22 (.951)	8.61 (1.07)	9.22 (2.275)	10.09 (2.661)	8.04 (2.549)	8.70 (2.245)	8.78 (2.593)	8.83 (2.188)	8.04 (1.846)	10.83 (2.674)	9.70 (1.428)	118.00 (15.303)
f-value	**45.13*** **P<0.000**	**46.91*** **P<0.000**	**5.94**** **P<0.005**	**1.95@** **P<0.151**	**0.88@** **P<0.420**	**0.55@** **P<0.581**	**0.27@** **P<0.762**	**2.64**** **P<0.080**	**11.79*** **P<0.000**	**0.22@** **P<0.805**	**13.64*** **P<0.000**	**0.18@** **P<0.838**

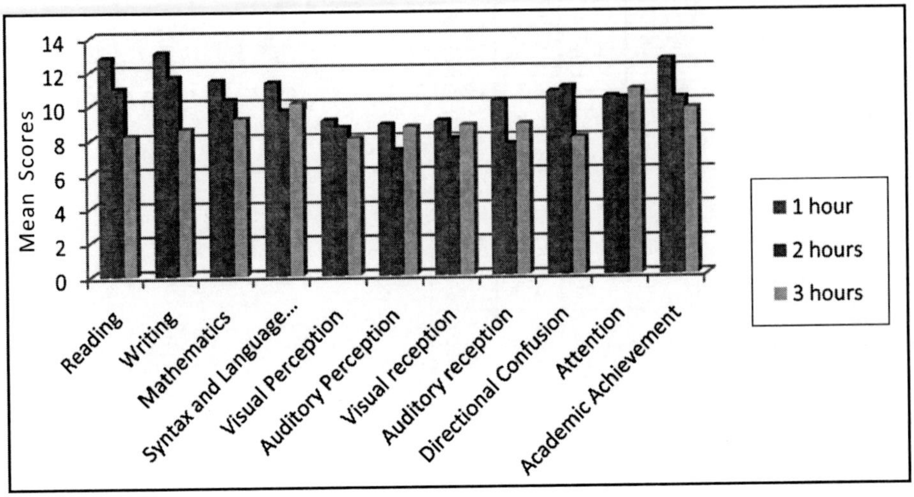

Fig. 4.7: Mean Scores of Problems Related to LD According to Time Spent per Day in SE Classes

SE Variables and Coping up of Problems by Children

The academic backwardness and pressure from teachers, parents and peers causes more stress for the student with LD. In order to assess how well students were able to manage with the problems related to LD and stress, the students who were attended SE classes were asked to rate their coping up of problems on a three point scale. Higher the score better coping up of problems by students.

Table 4.35 Shows the mean scores of coping up of problems related to LD as given by children.

Table 4.35

Mean Scores of Coping up of Problems Related to LD by Children and t-values

Children with LD n=(120)	Areas of Coping				
	Home	School/ Educational	Emotional	Social	Total
Attending SE	32.62 (5.533)	32.37 (5.511)	30.52 (5.385)	32.30 (5.366)	127.80 (20.120)
Not attending SE	26.37 (3.464)	26.92 (2.824)	26.33 (3.592)	26.27 (3.888)	105.85 (9.613)
t-values	**55.002*** P<0.000	**46.473*** P<0.000	**25.058*** P<0.000	**49.746*** P<0.000	**58.141*** P<0.000

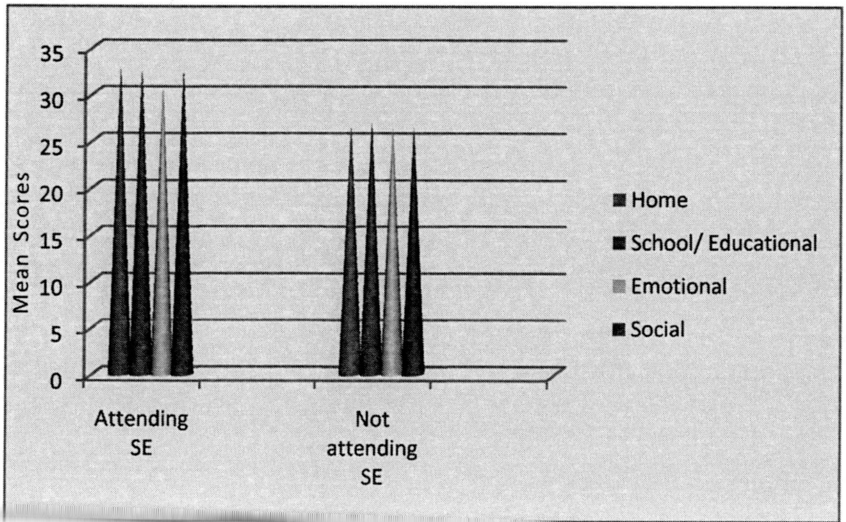

Fig. 4.8: Mean Scores of Coping up of Problems given by Children

From the table 4.35 and fig. 4.8, it is evident that in all areas, children attending special education perceived themselves as having more coping up of problems related to LD than those not attending special education classes. Renick and susan (1989), also reported that when children with LD compared their abilities with LD peers in resource rooms, they perceived high above their own performance. Attending special education classes helps children to understand their problems and methods of coping up of problems related to LD.

Table 4.36 shows the coping up of problems by students according to type of SE they were attending.

Table 4.36

Mean Scores of Coping up of Problems by Students according to Type of SE and t-values

S. No.	Type of SE	Mean Scores of Coping up of Problems				
		Home	School	Emotional	Social	Total
1.	Resources room	31.50 (5.88)	32.52 (5.72)	29.59 (4.88)	31.93 (5.01)	126.66 (18.79)
2.	Full time SE	32.59 (5.49)	32.23 (5.39)	31.39 (5.76)	32.65 (5.73)	128.87 (21.53)
	t value	**0.002@ P<0.968**	**0.041@ P<0.840**	**1.695@ P<0.198**	**0.262@ P<0.611**	**0.179@ P<0.674**

It divulges from table 4.36 that students did not differ significantly in coping up of problems in all areas i.e., home, social, emotional and school areas according to type of SE. The t-values were not significant in all areas of coping up of problems. However, a perusal of table 40 shows that comparatively, children who were attending full time special education classes were able to coping up with the problems better than those attending resource room classes.

Attending full time special education classes helps students to improve performance in academics as well as other areas of adjustment like home, social and emotional etc. Better adjustment helps to decrease stress and improves coping up capacity of the students. Baum *et al.,* (1998), reported that among the children with LD very few are attending special education or resource room classes. Boum *et.al.,* opined that up to 38 per cent of student population with LD was in need of intervention in different areas but that relatively few were actually receiving the needed interventions.

Hence, creating awareness among parents and teachers about intervention helps to decrease problems of LD and to increase coping up capacity by children with LD. Sunil *et al.,* (2011), reported that individualized remedial educational plan helps children with LD to cope up with disability and make get integrated in regular stream.

Table 4.37 shows the coping up of problems by students according to duration of SE classes.

Table 4.37

Mean Scores of Coping up of Problems by Students according to duration of Attending SE Classes and f-values

Duration of Attending Special Education	Mean Scores of Coping up of Problems				
	Home	School	Emotional	Social	Total
< 6 months	30.57 (4.72)	30.86 (4.63)	26.71 (4.92)	29.86 (4.34)	118.00 (15.64)
6-12 months	32.13 (6.16)	31.79 (6.21)	29.67 (5.35)	31.44 (5.60)	125.03 (21.62)
>12 months	35.00 (3.08)	34.71 (2.67)	34.79 (2.66)	35.93 (3.25)	140.43 (10.55)
f-value	**1.99@** **P<0.146**	**1.79@** **P<0.176**	**8.26**** **P<0.001**	**5.04*** **P<0.010**	**4.42@** **P<0.016***

From the table 4.37, it is known that, the mean scores of coping up of problems by children with LD differed significantly in the areas of emotional (f = 8.26), social (f = 5.04) and total score (f = 4.42) according to duration of SE. The f values were significant at .001 level. Children who were attending SE classes for more than 12 months duration have good coping scores than those who were attending below 12 months duration of SE classes.

Though, the f values were not significant in other areas of coping up viz., home and school, when the mean scores were observed the coping up of students seemed to be increased with the increase of duration of attending of SE classes. As the student started attending SE classes, slowly he/she shows improvement inperforming skills. Better performance in all areas decreases the problems associated with LD and improves the coping up capacity of students. These findings are in line with the results of the study of Roger and Saklotske (1985), who reported that children newly enrolled in SE classes differed significantly than those who attended SE classes for more than six months.

Table 4.38 shows the relationship between coping up of problems and time spent per day in SE classes.

Table 4.38

Mean Scores of Coping up of Problems by Students according to Time Spent in SE Classes per day and f-values

Time Spent per day in SE Classes	Mean Scores of Coping up of Problems				
	Home	School	Emotional	Social	Total
1 hour	31.47 (6.52)	31.15 (6.54)	28.59 (5.88)	30.76 (6.07)	121.97 (23.05)
2 hours	33.67 (2.52)	33.00 (3.61)	30.67 (1.15)	32.00 (2.00)	129.33 (8.33)
3 hours	34.17 (3.60)	34.09 (3.26)	33.35 (3.41)	34.61 (3.51)	136.22 (12.47)
f-value	**1.74@** **P<0.190**	**2.04@** **P<0.140**	**6.33*** **P<0.000**	**3.87**** **P<0.030**	**3.77**** **P<0.030**

Table 4.38, illustrates that students differed significantly in the coping up areas of adjustments like emotional (f=6.33), social (f=3.87) and total coping up score (f=3.77) according to time spent per day in special education classes. The f values were significant at .001level. With the increase of time spent in SE classes, the coping up scores of students also increased, which indicates better adjustment.

In an Indian study Madhuri *et al.*,(2001), reported that, with individualized education programme, most children learn to cope with disability and make get integrated in a regular stream.

Hence, parents and teachers must provide individualized education programme for children with LD not only to decrease problems of adjustments but also to improve coping up capacity of children.

SECTION VI

In this section determinants of outcome variables, viz., behaviour problems of children, parental perception of emotional reactions towards children's adjustments and coping up of problems by children with LDare explained.

Determinants of Outcome Variables

The independent variables of the study were child variables, parent variables and family variables. The dependent variables were behaviour problems among children as per teacher's perception, parent's perception of emotional reactions towards children's adjustments, problems elated LD and coping up of problems by children with LD.

Child variables of the study were child's age, gender, grade, birth order and IQ. Parent variables were fathers' education, fathers' occupation, mothers' education and mothers' occupation. Family variables of the study were type of family and family income.

Multiple linear regression analysis was performed to assess the determinants of outcome variables.

Determinants of Behaviour Problems of Sample Children

Multiple linear regression analysis was constructed to assess the major determinants of behaviour problems of sample children. Tables 4.39, 4.40 and 4.41 show the linear regression model and ANOVA of the regression analysis. The f value was significant (p<.000) which indicates the adequacy of the model.

Table 4.39

Model	R	R Square	Adjusted R Square	Std. Error of the Estimate
1	.692[a]	.479	.456	16.982

Table 4.40

ANOVA

Model	Sum of Squares	Df	Mean Square	f	Sig.
1. Regression	68280.416	11	6207.311	21.525	.000
Residual	74400.624	258	288.375		
Total		269			

(a) Dependent Variable: Teachers' perception of Students' Behaviour Problems Total Score.

(b) Predictors: (Constant), Gender, Age, Ordinal position, Class, IQ, Father education, Father occupation, Mother education, Mother occupation, Type of family, Income

Table 4.41, shows that among the selected independent variables, ordinal position, fathers' education, fathers' occupation, mothers' education and family income have shown significant contribution towards behaviour problems of children. The f values show that, these variables would be stronger determinants, good predictors for the behaviour problems among children as per teachers' perception. Rezique (1983), found that mother's educational level influenced children's academic achievement. It was reported that parents with poor educational levels may lack motivation and academic ambition, unable to help in their children's schoolwork and may have a low index of suspicion of their learning disabilities, delaying diagnosis and remedial teaching. Thus, if mothers were educated, they can identify the children learning disabilities at an early age and can help them to get remedial teaching. The data showed that first born children had more behaviour problems than later born children.

Table 4.41

Coefficients

Model		Unstandardized Coefficients		Standardized Coefficients	t	Sig.
		B	Std. Error	Beta		
	(Constant)	102.023	13.636		7.482	.000
	Gender	1.055	1.499	.038	.704	.482
	Age	-1.847	1.372	-.088	-1.347	.179
	Ordinal position	-3.953	2.206	.080	[illegible]	[illegible]
	Class	1.468	1.952	.050	.752	.453
1.	IQ	1.094	1.717	.034	.637	.525
	Father education	-2.275	.820	-.163	-2.776	.006
	Occupation	1.437	.381	.182	3.775	.000
	Mother education	-2.349	.387	-.346	-6.064	.000
	Occupation	1.665	.374	1.375	1.118	.523
	Type of family	-.461	3.176	-.007	-.145	.885
	Income	6.310	1.110	.343	5.691	.000

a. Dependent Variable: Teachers Perception of Students Behaviour Problems Total

Determinants of Parental Perception of Emotional Reactions towards Children Adjustments

To assess the major determinants of parental perception of emotional reactions towards children's adjustments multiple regression analysis was performed and results are presented in tables 4.42, 4.43 and 4.44.

Table 4.42

Model

Model	R	R Square	Adjusted R Square	Std. Error of the Estimate
1	.359[a]	.129	.092	25.424

Table 4.43

ANOVA

Model		Sum of Squares	Df	Mean Square	f	Sig.
	Regression	24688.236	11	2244.385	3.472	.000[b]
1	Residual	166769.927	258	646.395		
	Total	191458.163	269			

(a) Dependent Variable: Parental Perception of Emotional Reactions towards Children's Adjustments Total Score

(b) Predictors: (Constant), Gender, Age, Ordinal position, Class, IQ, Type of family, Income, Father education, Father occupation, Mother education, Mother occupation.

Table 4.44

Coefficients

Model		Unstandardized Coefficients		Standardized Coefficients	t	Sig.
		B	Std. Error	Beta		
	(Constant)	95.309	20.772		4.588	.000
	Gender	-3.993	3.165	-.075	-1.262	.208
	Age	2.457	1.938	.102	1.268	.206
	Ordinal position	-.734	3.395	-.014	-.216	.829
	Class	3.402	2.762	.101	1.232	.219
1	IQ	-1.797	2.801	-.042	-.642	.522
	Type of family	2.732	5.049	.032	.541	.589
	Income	-13.911	3.548	-.330	-3.921	.000
	Fathereducation	7.793	5.247	.228	1.485	.139
	Father occupation	-4.369	3.675	-.178	-1.189	.236
	Mother education	4.751	5.354	.131	.887	.376
	Mother occupation	.826	1.827	.039	.452	.651

(a) Dependent Variable: Parental Perception of Emotional Reactions towards Children's Adjustments Total Score

Table 4.42 and 4.43 show the linear regression model and ANOVA of the regression analysis. The f value was significant ($p<0.000$) which indicates the adequacy of the model.

Family income has shown significant contribution towards parental perception of stress reactions towards children's adjustments. As seen from the earlier tables with the increase of family income parents perceived more stressful reactions towards their children's adjustments.

Table 4.44 shows that among the selected independent variables, mother's education category has shown significant contribution towards children's adjustments. As the educational qualification of mothers increased the parental perception of stress towards children adjustments decreased.

Mothers with higher education qualification can understand the problems of LD children and may be the reason for perceiving less problems than mothers who had higher educational qualification. These findings were in line with the results of Raju and Rahamtulla (2000), who reported that parental education and occupation of the school children has significant influence on adjustments of children.

Determinants of Coping up of Problems Related to LD

Multiple linear regression analysis was constructed to assess the major determinants of coping up of problems as given by the child. Tables 4.45 and 4.46 show the linear regression model and ANOVA of the regression analysis. The f value was significant (p<.001) which indicates the adequacy of the model.

Table 4.45

Model

Model	R	R Square	Adjusted R Square	Std. Error of the Estimate
1	.598[a]	.358	.292	16.136

Table 4.46

ANOVA

Model		Sum of Squares	Df	Mean Square	f	Sig.
1	Regression	15667.789	11	1424.344	5.470	.001
	Residual	28121.536	108	260.385		
	Total	43789.325	119			

(a) Dependent Variable: Coping up of problems given by the child

(b) Predictors: (Constant), Gender, Age, Ordinal position, Class, IQ, Father education, Father occupation, Mother education, Mother occupation, type of family, Income.

Table 4.47 shows that among selected independent variables that is child, parent and family variables, ordinal position and mothers' education category has shown significant contribution towards coping up of problems by children.

As the education qualification of mothers' increased the coping up of problems of child also increased and similarly with the increase of the ordinal position of the child coping up of problems also seemed to be good.

Akhil and Tushar (2013), in a study on prevalence and pattern of learning disabilities in school children, reported that with the increases in number of siblings, there is decrease in number of positive cases of learning disabilities. As the birth order increases, not only the prevalence of LD in decreased but also the problems coping up capacity of children seemed to be increasing.

Table 4.47

Coefficients

Model		Unstandardized Coefficients		Standardized Coefficients	t	Sig.
		B	Std. Error	Beta		
	(Constant)	100.368	19.618		5.116	.000
	Gender	-.922	3.317	-.023	-.278	.782
	Age	1.737	2.340	.098	.742	.459
	Ordinal	4.144	2.099	.200	1.974	.051
	Class	2.780	3.524	.107	.789	.432
1	IQ	-1.316	2.425	-.058	-.543	.589
	Father Education	.304	1.121	.031	.271	.787
	Father Occupation	.073	.552	.012	.132	.896
	Mother Education	-1.664	.739	-.334	-2.251	.026
	Mother Occupation	-.070	.614	-.012	-.114	.909
	Type of family	.168	4.155	.003	.040	.968
	Income	-1.722	1.451	-.145	-1.187	.238

(a) Dependent Variable: Coping up of problems score given by the child

Contribution of LD Variables towards Coping up of Problems by Children

The LD variables of the study were type of LD (Listening, speaking, reading, writing, mathematics and reasoning problems) and duration of the problems. The dependent variable was total score of coping up of problems given by the children.

Table 4.48

Model

Model	R	R Square	Adjusted R Square	Std. Error of the Estimate
1	.585[a]	.342	.301	16.037

Table 4.49

ANOVA

Model	Sum of Squares	Df	Mean Square	f	Sig.
Regression	14983.662	7	2140.523	8.323	.000
Residual	28805.663	112	257.193		
Total	43789.325	119			

(a) Dependent Variable: Coping up of Problems Score

(b) Predictors: (Constant), Type of LD problem (listening, speaking, reading, writing, Mathematics, reasoning), duration of LD problem.

Table 4.50

Coefficients

Model		Unstandardized Coefficients		Standardized Coefficients	t-value	Sig.
		B	Std. Error	Beta		
	(Constant)	119.303	8.334		14.315	.000
	Listening	-3.156	2.267	-.124	-1.392	.167
	Speaking	1.839	1.507	.114	1.220	.225
1	Reading	6.655	2.140	-.245	-3.110	.002
	Writing	2.445	1.613	.149	1.516	.132
	Mathematics	.990	1.472	.064	.673	.502
	Reasoning	3.975	1.154	.312	3.444	.001
	Duration of LD	.427	.222	.157	1.922	.057

(a) Dependent Variable: coping up of problems Score

Regression analysis was conducted to assess the contribution of LD variables towards coping up of problems of sample children. Tables 4.48 and 4.49 show the linear regression analysis. The f value was significant (p<.000) which indicates the adequacy of model.

Table 4.50 shows that among the selected variables reading (t=3.110, p<0.002) Reasoning (t=3.44, p<.001) and duration of LD (t=1.922, p<.057) have shown significant contribution towards children's coping up of problems.

Contribution of SE Variables towards Coping up of Problems by Children

To predict the impact of SE related variables that determine coping up of problems given by the child, regression analysis was constructed. The SE variables of the study were type of SE, duration of SE and time spent per day in SE.

Table 4.51 and table 4.52 show the linear regression model and ANOVA of the regression analysis. The f value was significant (p<.001) which indicates the adequacy of the model.

Table 4.53 shows that among the selected independent variables duration of SE and time spent per day in SE classes have shown significant contribution towards coping up of problems by children (t=1.79, p<0.079 and t=3.295, p<0.002 respectively). Duration of time spent in SE classes also showed contribution (t=1.792, p<0.079).

When the duration of SE classes is for longer time and if children spend more time per day in SE classes, the children's coping up capacity increasedmay be because of special and individual care taken by the special educator. Similar views were reported by Vaughn and Klinger (1998), who found that majority of students with LD preferred to receive specialized instructions outside the general education classroom for part of the school day and students also liked resource rooms because they get help to do their work. This helps to improve coping up capacity for children to deal with problems related to LD.

Table 4.51

Model

Model	R	R Square	Adjusted R Square	Std. Error of the Estimate
1	.547[a]	.300	.235	17.599

Table 4.52

ANOVA

Model		Sum of Squares	Df	Mean Square	f	Sig.
1	Regression	7158.769	5	1431.754	4.623	.001
	Residual	16724.831	54	309.719		
	Total	23883.600	59			

(a) Dependent Variable: coping up of problems score

(b) Predictors: (Constant), Type of special education, Duration of SE, Time spent in SE class per day.

Table 4.53

Coefficients

Model		Unstandardized Coefficients		Standardized Coefficients	t	Sig.
		B	Std. Error	Beta		
1	(Constant)	101.899	19.584		5.203	.000
	Type of special education	-19.814	7.023	-.496	-2.821	.007
	Duration of special education	7.884	4.400	.229	1.792	.079
	Time spent in special education	12.676	3.846	.608	3.295	.002

(a. b.) Dependent Variable: coping up of problems score

Madhuri *et al.,* (2001), also reported that with Individualized Remedial Education Plan (IEP) most children learn to cope up with the disability and may get integrated in a regular steam. Hence, early identification of LD problems and early intervention help in bringing out better coping up capacity among children with LD.

The analysis of results discussed in section I to VI revealed the following major findings.

Major Findings of the Study

- Comparatively the prevalence of learning disability was more among boys than girls in sample students.
- Majority of normal achievers (50 per cent) were second born and with regard to children with LD majority (42.5 per cent) were first born.
- Majority of children with LD had average intelligence on par with normal achievers.
- Majority of parents of LD children were illiterates and had low occupational status and were from middle income group.
- Majority of sample children, both normal achievers (90 per cent) and children with LD (88.3 per cent) were from nuclear families.
- Comparatively children with LD had more behaviour problems in all areas than those without LD according to teacher's perception.
- Parents of children with LD perceived more stressful emotional reactions of about their children's adjustments.
- Majority of the children were identified having LD at the age of 8 years based on class work observation. Hence, teachers can be trained in early identification of children with LD.
- Teachers and parents perceived more problems in dyslexia, dyscalculia and dysgraphia than other problems related LD.
- Significant correlation was found for the problems related to LD as given by parents and teachers ($r=0.15$ and $p<0.044$).
- Ninety per cent of sample children who were attending special education classes were attending the special classes based on the suggestion from the class teacher.
- Majority of children (60 per cent) were attending the special education classes from 6 months to one year period.
- More than half of children attending SE were spending time in SE classes for 3 hours per day.
- Comparatively children attending SE classes have more coping up capacity of problems than those who were not attending SE classes.
- Children with and without LD differed significantly in all areas of behaviour problems.
- Comparatively teachers perceived more problems for children with LD than those without LD.
- Sample children differed significantly in certain areas of behaviour problems according to gender, age, birth order and IQ as per teachers' perception.

- Comparatively teachers perceived more problems for girlsthan boys among children with and without LD in home area.
- Among children with LD it was found that with increase in age theintensity of behaviour problems decreased significantly.
- Comparatively the mean scores of behaviour problems for first bornchildren were more than for later born.
- The mean scores of problems in academic area have decreased with increase of IQ for both the groups of children, i.e. with and without LD.

- Children with LD differed significantly from children without LD in all areas of adjustments as per parent's perception of emotional reactions. Comparatively parents of children with LD perceived more stress than those of without LD.
    - As the age increased parents of normal achieving children perceived less stress in all areas of adjustments and parents of children with LD comparatively expressed more stress.
    - Parents' perception of stress was comparatively low for later born than first born children.
    - Irrespective of problems of LD parents perceived less stress for those children who had above average intelligence.
- Comparatively parents with higher educational qualification perceived more problems towards their children's adjustments than those with lower education qualification.
- Comparatively children of Govt./Private employees and those from families where father's occupation was agriculture seemed to have perceived more problems than those parents whose occupations were business and daily labor work.
- When children with LD were considered, children did not differ significantly according to type of LD in all areas of behaviour problems except that of social area as per teacher's perception.
    - Children with LD had less problems in social area which showed good social adjustment. If parents and teachers encourage social skills among children with LD they may excel in social functioning though, they were backward in academic area.
- When different types LD such as listening, speaking, reading, writing, mathematics and reasoning were considered, comparatively parents perceived less stress when the child has problems related to reasoning.

- When relationship among SE variables and behaviour problems as per teachers' perception was considered, children with LD attending SE did not differ in all problem areas.
    - ❖ Comparatively children who were attending full time SE class have less problems than those who were attending resource room classes.
    - ❖ Comparatively teachers perceived less problems for the students who were attending SE for around 3 hours a day, than those for students who were attending less than 3 hours.
- When relationship among SE variables and parental perception of emotional reactions towards children's adjustments was considered, the mean scores showed that parents perceived less stress for children who were attending full time SE classes than those attending classes in resource rooms.
- When relationship among SE variables and problems related LD such as reading, writing, Mathematics, syntax, visual and auditory perception, visual and auditory reception, directional confusion, attention and academic achievement were consideredsample students differed significantly according to SE variables.
    - ❖ The magnitude of problems related LD were decreased when duration of SE classes increased.
    - ❖ Students who were attending SE classes for more than 12 months were having less problems than those who were attending SE classes for 6-12 months and 6 months.
    - ❖ The magnitudes of problems were reduced when students have spent more time per day in SE classes.
- When relationship among SE variables and coping up of problems related to LD by children was considered, children differed significantly according to type of SE, duration of SE and time spent per day in SE classes.
    - ❖ Comparatively children who were attending full time special education classes were able to cope upwith the problems better than those attending resource room classes.
    - ❖ Children who were attending SE classes for more than 12 months duration have good coping than those who were attending below 12 months duration of SE classes.
    - ❖ With the increase of time spent in SE classes per day, the coping up scores of students also increased, which indicates better coping up capacity.

- Among the selected independent variables ordinal position, fathers' education, fathers' occupation, mothers' education and family income have shown significant contribution towards behaviour problems of children, which shows that, these variables would be stronger determinants, good predictors for the behaviour problems among children as per teachers' perception.
- Among the selected independent variables mother's education category has shown significant contribution towards children's adjustments.
    - ❖ As the educational qualification of mothers increased the adjustment problems among children have decreased. Mothers with higher education qualification can understand the problems of LD children and may by the reason for less problems for children whose mothers had higher educational qualification.
- Among selected independent variables that is child, parent and family variables, ordinal position and mothers' education category has shown significant contribution towards children's coping up of problems related to LD.
    - ❖ As the education qualification of mothers increased the coping up of problems of child also increased and similarly with the increase of the ordinal position of the child coping up of problems also seemed to be high.
- Among the selected LD variables, reading, reasoning and duration of LD have shown significant and positive contribution towards children's coping up of problems.
- Among the selected SE variables, duration of SE and time spent per day in SE classes have shown significant contribution towards coping up of problems by children.
    - ❖ When the duration of SE classes is for longer time and if children spend more time per day in SE classes, the children's coping up capacity increased may be because of special and individual care taken by the special educator.
- Early identification of LD problems and early intervention help in bringing out better coping up capacity among children with LD.

Implications

- The findings of the study showed that teachers perceived behaviour problems among both children with and without LD. However, comparatively children with LD had more problems than normal achievers. Among children with LD, those who were attending special education classes have less problems than those not attending SE classes. Hence, parents and teachers can be educated about significance of special education to children with LD.

- The results of present study showed that parents perceived more stressful emotional reactions towards children's adjustments especially for children with LD than the parents of children without LD. Parents should be provided with awareness programmes about the problems related to LD and they also should be given emotional support programmes through group counseling. If parents understand the problems related to LD and if they perceive the reasons for poor academic performance and social dysfunction, they can provide emotional support to children to cope up with problems related to LD.
- When children with LD attending special education in resource rooms and full time SE classes were compared, children with full time SE classes have better coping up of problems than those attending resource rooms. With the increase of time spent in SE classes, the children showed better adjustments. This clearly shows the importance of full time special education classes for children with LD.

  From the observations made by the investigator it was found that there are no full time SE schools in the study area except that in Hyderabad and Secendrabad cities (At present in Telangana state). Hence, there is a dire need of establishment of special schools for children with LD. Policy makers and NGOs can make efforts in this regard.
- The investigator while identifying children with LD from normal schools, experienced that majority of the teachers have lack of awareness about the concept of learning disability. If teachers are trained, then they can identify children with LD at an early age which will be helpful to provide early remedial teaching. The concept of identification of LD can be incorporated into the teacher training modules. A special B.Ed programme with learning disability is needed in present AP state as no such course is available.

As the problem of learning disability among children has been increasing globally and also in our country, special education schools, special education training and teachers who have knowledge about LD are imperative.

Limitations of the Study

- Obtaining sample of children with LD in normal schools involves more time and effort. Hence, the sample size for children with LD was limited to 120.

- Though, resource rooms are officially present in normal schools, very few children were available in those schools. Hence, sample for children attending resource room were also limited.
- Research studied with much larger sample size would be required to ensure appropriate generalization of the findings of the study.
- Special schools for LD children are not available in present AP state. Hence, the sample for children attending full time special education classes were selected from special school in Hyderabad and Secunderabad cities. Hence, replication of the study at different stage which have SE schools would enable better generalizability of findings of the study.

Suggestions for Further Research

- Similar study can be conducted on problems of children in early grades of high school
- It would be worthwhile to conduct inter-state comparative study ofimpact of SE on LD children.
- Coping up strategies by parents of children with LD can be studied
- It would be worthwhile to investigate in depth study on a specific learning disability and its relation with academic achievement.

5

Summary and Conclusion

The middle childhood which extends from six to eleven years is crucial stage in children's life during which children enter elementary school.Each period during childhood is marked by basic biological and cognitive changes, as well as changes in the social surroundings where children's daily lives unfold. During elementary school age, children learn about the wider world and master improved athletic abilities, participation in games with rules, more logical thought processes, mastery of basic literacy skills, and advances in self-understanding, morality and friendship (Berk, 2003). Children grasp the concepts of space and time in more logical, practical ways. They gain a better understanding of cause and effect, and of calendar time. At this stage, children are eager to learn and accomplish more complex skills like reading, writing, telling time etc.

Learning disability is a general term that refers to a heterogeneous group of disorders manifested by significant difficulties in the acquisition and use of listening, speaking, reading, writing, reasoning, or mathematical abilities. These disorders are intrinsic to the individual and presumed to be due to central nervous system dysfunction, and may occur across the lifespan. Problems in self-regulatory behaviours, social perception, and social interaction may exist with learning disabilities but do not by themselves constitute a learning disability.

Special education or special needs education is the education of students with special needs in a way that addresses the students' individual differences and needs. Ideally, this process involves the individually planned and systematically monitored arrangement of teaching procedures, adapted equipment and materials, accessible settings, and other interventions designed to help learners with special needs achieve a higher level of personal self-sufficiency and success in school and community than would be available if the student were only given access to a typical classroom education.

The special education classroom may be the only place where these children will be equipped with stress management skills which will become increasingly more important as the pressures to achieve academically increase.

In India around 13-14 per cent of all school children suffer from learning disorders. Unfortunately most teachers fail to lend a sympathetic ear to the problems of children. As a result these children are branded as failures. Despite the fact that, the learning disabilities which includes a group of disorders like listening, speaking, reading, writing and mathematics etc is a known class room disorders, it has not reached its optimum awareness levels in the schools in our country.

On the basis of the review of earlier literature and also basing on the general observation of children's adjustments and impact of special education on management of problems, the following objectives were formulated:

1. To identify the sample children with learning disability using Identification of Learning Disability Inventory (LDDI, Hammill and Bryant 1998)
2. To compare IQ, Behaviour problems and Parental Perception of Emotional Reaction towards Children's Adjustments of children with and without Learning disability.
3. To assess the relationship among demographic variables and teachers' perception of behaviour problems among children.
4. To assess the Relationship among Demographic Variables and Parents' Perception of Emotional Reactions towards Children's Adjustments.
5. To assess the relationship among LD Variables, Behaviour Problems and Parental Perception of Emotional Reactions towards Children's Adjustment.
6. To assess the Relationship among SE Variables, Behaviour Problems, Parental Perception of Emotional Reactions towards Children's Adjustment and Coping up of Problems by Children.
7. To find out the Determinants of outcome Variables.

The variables of the study were Child Variables (Age, Gender, Birth order, Grade/Class, IQ), Parent Variables – (Father's Educational Qualification, Father's Occupation, Mother's Educational Qualification, Mother's Occupation), Family Variables (Type of family and Income), LD variables - (Type of LD-Listening, Speaking, Reading, Writing, Mathematics and Reasoningand Duration of LD Problem),Special Education Variables (Type of Special Education, Duration of attending special education, Time spends per day in special education classes), Parental perception of

Emotional Reactions towards Children's Adjustments,Teachers' perception of Behaviour Problems of Children, Problems Related to Learning Disability and Coping up of problems related to learning disability from children's perspective.

For measuring the above mentioned different variables of the study the investigator developed three tools and adapted two tools. The following are the tools developed/adapted to collect the information from three types of subjects–Children (Normal achievers and children with learning disabilities), Parents and teachers.

1. Learning Disability Diagnostic Inventory – (Developed by Hammilland Bryant 1998)
2. Standard Raven's Progressive Matrices (SRPM) Test (Developed by Raven, 1976)
3. Behaviour Problems Check list (Developed by Anuradha and Bharathi, 2004 and adapted for present study)
4. General Information Schedule.
5. Parental Perception of Children's Adjustments Scale.
6. Checklist for Problems Related to Learning Disability for Parents' and Teachers'.
7. Check List for Assessment of Coping up of Problems of Learning Disability.

A pilot study was conducted, on a sample of 50 children studying 3rd, 4th and 5th standard who were selected randomly from schools at Hyderabad and Tirupati. Ten schools were identified randomly from each place and 25 children with specific learning disability were identified using Learning Disability Diagnostic Inventory. Twenty five normal achievers were identified randomly from same classes from which LD were identified. The tools developed and adapted were administered on the pilot study sample. Item analysis was performed and the reliability was established using test-re test and split half reliability methods. The validity was established with help of judgment of experts from different fields like Child Development, Psychology and Special Education.

The data for final study was collected from children studying in 3rd, 4th and 5th grades in three places of state i.e., Hyderabad, Nellore and Chittoor Districts representing one district from different regions of the state i.e. Rayalaseema, Costal and Telangana. Five revenue divisions were selected randomly and total 15 revenue divisions among three districts were selected. Within each revenue division 4 schools were selected randomly and then from each school children with learning disabilities were selected purposively. Normal achievers from same class were selected using systematic stratified random sampling technique. Thus, 150 Normal achievers, 120 children with learning disability (60 children who were attending special education and 60 children who were not attending special education) constituted the sample. Mothers and teachers of the selected children were the sub-samples of the study.

The subjects were administered with relevant tools, by following the procedure for administration, after establishing a good rapport.

The data thus collected were processed both qualitatively and quantitatively using appropriate statistical methods. To study the influence of independent variables on dependent variables't' test and 'f' test were calculated. Karl Pearson's Coefficient of Correlation was computed to find the relationship between parents' perception and teachers' perception of problems related to LD. Multiple linear regression was performed to estimate the determinants of outcome variables.

The results of analysis were discussed against the already available literature and the following were some of the salient findings of the investigation bearing in mind the objectives, and methodological limitations:

- Comparatively the prevalence of learning disability was more among boys than girlsand among first born children.
- Majority of children with LD had average intelligence on par with normal achievers.
- Comparatively children with LD had more behaviour problems in all areas than those without LD according to teacher's perception.
- Parents of children with LD perceived more stressful emotional reactions of about their children's adjustments.
- Teachers and parents perceived more problems in dyslexia, dyscalculia and dysgraphia than other problems related LD.
- More than half of children attending SE were spending SE classes 3 hours per day.
- Comparatively teachers perceived more problems for children with LD than those without LD.
- Sample children differed significantly in certain areas of behaviour problems according to gender, age, birth order and IQ as per teachers' perception.
    - ❖ Comparatively teachers perceived more problems for girls than boys among children with and without LD in home area.
    - ❖ Among children with LD it was found that with increase in age the intensity of behaviour problems decreased significantly.

- Comparatively the mean scores of behaviour problems for first born children were more than for later born.
- The mean scores of problems in academic area have decreased with increase of IQ for both the groups of children, i.e. with and without LD.

- Children with LD differed significantly from children without LD in all areas of adjustments as per parent's perception of emotional reactions. Comparatively parents of children with LD perceived more stress than those of without LD.
  - As the age increased parents of normal achieving children perceived less stress in all areas of adjustments and parents of children with LD comparatively expressed more stress.
  - Parents' perception of stress was comparatively low for later born than first born children.
  - Irrespective of problems of LD parents perceived less stress for those children who had above average intelligence
- When children with LD were considered children did not differ significantly according to type of LD in all areas of behaviour problems except that of social area as per teacher's perception.
- When relationship among SE variables and parental perception of emotional reactions towards children's adjustments was considered, the mean scores showed that parents perceived less stress for children who were attending full time SE classes than those attending classes in resource rooms.
- When relationship among SE variables and coping up of problems related to LD by children was considered, children differed significantly according to type of SE, duration of SE and time spent per day in SE classes.
  - Comparatively children who were attending full time special education classes were able to cope up with the problems better than those attending resource room classes.
  - Children who were attending SE classes for more than 12 months duration have good coping than those who were attending below 12 months duration of SE classes.
  - With the increase of time spent in SE classes per day, the coping up scores of students also increased, which indicates better coping up capacity.
- Among the selected independent variables ordinal position, fathers' education, fathers' occupation, mothers' education and family income have shown significant contribution towards

behaviour problems of children,which shows that, these variables would be stronger determinants, good predictors for the behaviour problems among children as per teachers' perception.

- Among the selected independent variables mother's education category has shown significant contribution towards children's adjustments.
- Among selected independent variables that is child, parent and family variables, ordinal position and mothers' education category has shown significant contribution towards children's coping up of problems related to LD.
- Among the selected LD variables, reading, reasoning and duration of LD have shown significant and positive contribution towards children's coping up of problems.
- Among the selected independent SE variables, duration of SE and time spent per day in SE classes has shown significant contribution towards coping up of problems by children.
- Early identification of LD problems and early intervention help in bringing out better coping up capacity among children with LD.

Thus, the results had shown that when compared to normal achievers with learning disability had more adjustment problems. Parents also perceived more stressful emotional reactions for children with LD. Attending special education classes by children with LD helped teachers and parents to perceive less problems and also better coping up capacity by children with LD.As there is no full time SE school for children with LD is available in the study area.

Bibliography

Akhil, D. and Tushar, J. (2013). Prevalence and Pattern of Learning Disabilities in School Children. *Delhi Psychiatry Journal*, 16(2), 386-390.

Amanda, M., Vander, H., Joseph, C.W. and Gale, N. (2003). Development and Validation of a Process for Screening Referrals to Special Education. School Psychology Review, 32.

Anderson and George (1998). Teaching Learning Disabled Students in the General Education Classroom. *Journal of Learning Disabilities*, 6(3), 21.

Andreassi and Cristia, L. (2007). The Relationship Among Behaviour, Social Cognition, and Peer Acceptance in School-identified Children with Learning Disabilities. *Journal of Learning Disabilities*, 7 (3), 23.

Arwood, S.H. (2005). Reading Instruction for Elementary Age Students with Emotional and Behavioural Disorders: Academic and Behavioural Outcomes, *Journal of Exceptional Children*, 72(1), 7-27.

Atkins and Tina (2008). A Case Study Examining the Collaboration Between General Education and Special Education Teachers in Inclusive Classrooms. *Journal of Learning Disabilities*, 10 (2), 10.

24th Annual Report to Congress (2002). Retrieved from https://www2.ed.gov/ about/reports/annual/osep/2002/toc-execsum.pdf

Banerji, M. and Ronald, A.D. (1995). A Study of the Effects of an Inclusion Model on Students with Specific Learning Disabilities. *Journal of Learning Disabilities*, 28(8), 511-522.

Barry, L.M. (2004). A Comparison of Teacher, Peer, and Self-monitoring with Curriculum-based Measurement in Reading Among Students with Learning Disabilities. *Journal of Learning Disability*, 25 (1), 25-27.

Baum, D.D. (1998). Resource Teacher Perceptions of the Prevalence of Social Dysfunction Among Students with Learning Disabilities, *Journal of Learning Disabilities*, 21(6), 380-381.

Berk, L.E. (2003). *Child Development* (6th ed.). Boston: Allyn and Bacon, 25-27.

Betty, A.H. and Kauffman, J.M. (1995). How does Observational Learning Affect the Behaviour of Students with Emotional or Behavioural Disorders – A Review of Research. *Journal of Special Education*, 29(1), 45-71.

Bowe, H. (2005). *Making Inclusion Work*. Upper Saddle River, N.J: Prentice Hall.

Bradshaw, S. (2001). Structural Adjustment to Social Adjustment. Journal of Psychology, 8(2), 188-207.

Brayan, T.H. (1974). Learning Disabled Children's Comprehension of Non Verbal Communication. *Journal of Learning Disabilities*, 10, 501-506.

Bruce, G.T. (1980). Visual Memory Structures in Learning Disabled Children. University School of Education. *Journal of Learning Disability*, 41(5), 299.

Bryan, T.M. (1974). Peer Popularity of Learning Disabled Children. *Journal of Learning Disability*, 7(10), 621-625.

Carlson, E. and Parshall, L. (1996). Academic, Social, and Behavioural Adjustment for Students Declassified from Special Education. *Journal of Exceptional Children*, 63 (1), 89-100.

Carol, A.B., and Vogler, C. (2001). The Critical Limits of Embodiment: Disability Criticism, Public Culture, 13 (3), 349-357.

Carol, W.S. and Watson. B.L. (1992). The Prevalence of Depressive Symptoms in Children with Learning Disabilities. *Journal of Learning Disabilities*, 25(4), 258-264.

Carolyn, R.M., Top of Form.

Cathy, M.R. and Symons, D.K. (2004). The Bidirectional Relationship between Achievement and Externalizing Behaviour Problems of Students with Learning Disabilities. *Journal of Learning Disability*, 28(1), 817. fromhttp://ldx.sagepub.com/content/28/1/8.abstract

Chandramuki, S., Indiramma, V.K.S., and Narasimha, M.V. (2012). Attitudes of Parents towards Children with Specific Learning Disabilities, *Journal of Learning Disability*, 23(1), 63-68.

Chapman and James, W. (1988). Cognitive-motivational Characteristics and Academic Achievement of Learning Disabled Children: A Longitudinal Study. *Journal of Educational Psychology*, 80(3), 357-365.

Chapman and James, W. (1999). Learning Disabilities, Locus of Control, and Mother Attitudes. Journal of Educational Psychology, 71(2), 250-258.

Cheryy, G., and Joyce, M. (1996). Coping with School Stress: A Comparison of Adolescents with and without Learning Disabilities. *Journal of Learning Disabilities*, 29(3), 287-296.

Clements, S. (1966). Minimal Brain Dysfunction in Children, Public Health Service Bulletin, U.S. Department of Health Education and Welfare. Retrieved from http://books.google.co.in/books_id.

Cortiella, C. (2009). The State of Learning Disabilities. National Center for Learning Disabilities, New York. Retrieved from http://www.specialednews.com/ learning-problems/special-education-learning-disabilities.htm.

Daniels, R.I. (1996). The Co-existence of Artistic Talent and Dyslexia. Columbia University Teachers College. *Dissertation Abstracts International*, 57(7), 309.

David, F.W., Richard. D., Saudargas. A., and Zanolli, K. (1990). LD Children's Regular Classroom Behaviour before and after Identification and Placement. *Journal of Learning Disability*, 13(3), 196-204.

Denise, D.V. (2001). Mediators of the Risk for Problem Behaviour in Children with Language Learning Disabilities. *Journal of Learning Disabilities*, 15(2), 23-27.

Deshpande, C.G., and Ojha, J.M. (2002). Indian Norms for Raven's Standard Progressive Matrices: A Normative Study in Delhi and Maharashtra.

Dorit, R. (1991). Individual Differences in the Self-image of Adolescents with Learning Disabilities: The Roles of Severity, Time of Diagnosis, and Parental Perceptions. *Journal of Learning Disability*, 24(10), 602-611.

Duncan, D. and Matson, J.L. (1999). The Relationship of Self-injurious Behaviour and Aggression to Social Skills in Persons with Severe and Profound Learning Disability. Journal of Learning Disability. 10(2), 210-213.

Dyson, L.L. (1996). The Experiences of Families of Children and Adolescents with Learning Disabilities: Parental Stress, Family Functioning and Sibling Self-concept. *Journal of Learning Disabilities*, 29(3), 280-286.

Eccles (1999). The Development of Children Age 6-14. The Future of Children, 9(2), 30-14.

Edwin, E. (2002). Watering up the Curriculum for Adolescents with Learning Disabilities, Part I: Goals of the Knowledge Dimension, 22.

Elana, E.R. (1997). The Concomitance of Learning Disabilities and Emotional/Behavioural Disorders – A Conceptual Model. *Journal of Learning Disabilities*, 30(3), 245-263.

Elias, A. and Brahm, N. (2010). Teachers' Attitudes towards Integration/Inclusion: A Review of the Literature. *Journal of Learning Disabilities*, 25(1), 129-147.

Erik Erikson (1979). Theory of Psychological Development. Retrieved from http://www.google.co.in/sarch/site.

Gandhimathi, U.J.O., Gnanajane, J. and Eljo. (2009). Awareness about Learning Disabilities among the Primary School Teachers, *Cauvery Research Journal*, 13(1), 21-26.

Gartner, A., and Lipsy, D.K. (1997). Inclusion and School Reform: Transforming America's Classrooms. Brookes Publishing Company.

Gary, M.S. and Doran, C.F. (1998). A Comparison of the Social Competencies of Learning Disabled and Low Achieving Elementary - Aged Children, *Journal of Special Education,* 23(1), 29-42.

Gathercole, S.E., Alloway. T.P., Willis, C. and Adams, A.M. (2005). Working Memory in Children with Reading Disabilities. *Journal of Exceptional Child Psychology,* 93(3), 265-81.

Gitanjali, S. (2004). A Comparative Study of the Personality Characteristics of Primary School Students with Learning Disabilities and their Non Learning Disabled Peers. *Journal of Learning Disability.* 27(3), 127-140.

Good, C.V. (1959). Dictionary of Education, New York: McGraw-Hill Book Company, 6.

Goodman, L. (1990). Time and Learning in the Special Education Classroom. Albany, State University of New York Press, 122.

Grace, T. and Janet, W. (2012). Learning Support for Students with Learning Difficulties in India and Australia: Similarities and Differences. *Journal International Education,* 11(1), 3-21.

Green, R.J., Clopton, J.R. and pope, A.W. (1996). Understanding Gender Differences in Referral of Children in Mental Health Services. *Journal of Emotional and Behaviour Disorders,* 4(3), 182-190.

Greenwood, C.R. (1991). Longitudinal Analysis of Time, Engagement, and Achievement in at-risk versus Non-risk Students, 57 (6), 521-35.

Hana Tur-Kaspa and Bryan, T. (1995). Teachers' Ratings of the Social Competence and School Adjustment of Students with ld in Elementary and Junior High School. *Journal of Learning Disability,* 28(1), 44-52.

Hicks, B. (2011). Disabled Children Excluded from Education. BBC Online. Retrieved from. https://mail.google.com/ssc/state

Expand+Hornstra, L. and Denesser, E. (2010). Teacher Attitudes toward Dyslexia: Effects on Teacher Expectations and the Academic Achievement of Students with Dyslexia. *Journal of Disability,* 43(6), 515-529. Retrieved from https://mail.google.com/ssc/state

Hurlock, E.B. (1980). *Developmental Psychology,* A Life Span Approach, Edition 5, Hill Education Publishers, 80-83.

Individuals with Disabilities Education Act, IDEA, (2004). Retrieved from study.com/.../idea-individuals-with-disabilities-education-act-history-and

International Dyslexia Association, (2006). Retrieved from https://en.wikipedia.org/ wiki/ International_Dyslexia_Association.

Jain, P. (1972). Agra Psychological Association Cell, New Delhi.

James, B.H., *et al.*, (2001). Executive Impairment Determines ADHD Medication Response: Implications for Academic Achievement. *Journal of Abnormal Psychology*. http://ldx.sagepub.com/content/44/2/196.abstract

James, D.M. (2002). Longitudinal Research on the Behavioural Characteristics of Children with Learning Disabilities. *Journal of Learning Disabilities*, 22 (3), 141-150.

James, Q.A., Sally, M., Adams, A., and Sheila, L. (1988). Integrated Classroom versus Resource Model: Academic Viability and Effectiveness. *Exceptional Children*, 17 (2), 57-58.

Janet, W.L. (2000). Enhancing the Quality of Mathematics for Students with Learning Disabilities. Illustrations from Subtraction. *Learning Disabilities - A* Multidisciplinary *Journal*, 11(2) 30-31.

Jorgensen, C.M. (1998). Restructuring High School for all Students: Taking Inclusion to the Next Level. Baltimore: Paul H. Brooks Publishing co.

Juan, E.J. (2011). Gender Ratio and Cognitive Profiles in Dyslexia - A Cross-national Study. *Journal of Learning Disability*, 24(7), 729-747.

Judith, W. (2004). Do Peer Relationships Foster Behavioural Adjustment in Children with Learning Disabilities. *Journal of Applied Psychology*, 27, 21.

Judith, W. and Michal, S. (1998). Expand+Knowledge about and Preoccupation with Reading Disabilities - A Delicate Balance. *Journal of Learning Disabilities*, 26(4), 132-140.

Juvonen and George. (1992). Social Adjustment of Children with and without Learning Disabilities in Integrated Classrooms. *Journal of Educational Psychology*, 84(3), 322-330.

Kamala, R. (2014). Specific Learning Disabilities in India - Rights, Issues and Challenges. *Indian Journal of Applied Research*, 4 (5), 604-605.

Karande, S., Sholapurwala, R., and Kulkarni, M. (2011). Managing Specific Learning Disability in Schools in India. *Indian Pediatric Journal*, 48(7), 515-20.

Karen, Z.S., and Miller, D. (2006). Teachers, Schools and Society: A Brief Introduction to Education with Bind-in Online Learning Center, McGraw-Hill, 48-49.

Kasinath, H.M.(1990). Adjustment between Migrated Hindi and Non-Hindi Speaking Students Studying in Jawahar Navodaya Vidyalayas. The Progress of Education, 8-10.

Katsafanas and Jodi, D. (2007). The Roles and Responsibilities of Special Education Teachers. *Journal of Learning Disabilities*, 10(2), 30.

Kausar, R. and Munir, B. (2008). Pakistani Adolescents' Socio-emotional Adjustment: Comparison of Single Parent Adolescents with those from intact Families. *Indian Journal of Psychology and Mental Health*, 1 (2), 9-21.

Kavita, K., Sharmila, D., and Darshan, N. (2012). Identifying Children with Specific Learning Disabilities. *Journal of Learning Disabilities*, 2(8), 249-255.

Konstantareas, M.M. and Homatidis, S. (1989). Parental Perception of Learning-disabled Children's Adjustment Problems and Related Stress. *Journal of Abnormal Child Psychology*, 17(2), 177-86.

Kulshrestha, S.P. (1979). Educational Psychology. Meerut, India: Loyal Book Depot.

Lana, C.Z. and Nancy, L.H. (2008). Parents and Youth with Learning Disabilities Perceptions of Relationships and Communication. *Journal of Learning Disability*, 41(6), 524-534. Retrieved from http://ldx.sagepub.com/content/ 41/6/524.abstract

Lardieri, L., Blacher and Swansan, L. (2000). Sibling Relationships and Parent Stress in Families of Children with and without Learning Disabilities. *Journal of Learning Disabilities*, 25, 105.

Lawrence, L. (1994). The Social Adjustment and Self-concept of Adults with Learning Disabilities. *Journal of Learning Disability*, 27(9), 598-605.

Lerner, S. (2000). Learning and Behavioural Characteristics of Individuals with Learning Disabilities. Retrieved from http:www.naset.org/ file admin/user_ upload/LD_Report/ issue_3_LD_report_characteristic_of_L.

Leslie, M.F.(1986). Coping and Defense Mechanisms of Mothers of Learning Disabled Children. *Journal of Learning Disability*, 19 (1), 8-11.

Lily, L.D. (1996). The Experiences of Families of Children with Learning Disabilities: Parental Stress, Family Functioning, and Sibling Self-concept. *Journal of Learning Disability*, 29 (3), 280-286.

Lily, L.D. (2006). Fathers and Mothers of School-age Children with Developmental Disabilities: Parental Stress, Family Functioning, and Social Support. *European Journal of Special Needs Education*, 19(2), 27-29.

Lisa, K., Chandra, J.F., and Vince, J.R. (2010). Inclusion Classrooms and Teachers: A Survey of Current Practices. *Journal of Learning Disabilities*, 34(4), 251-256.

Lisette, H., Eddie, D.J.B., Linda, D.B., and Marinus,V. (2010). Teachers' Attitudes towards Dyslexia - Effects on Teachers' Expectations and the Academic Achievement of Students with Dyslexia. *Journal of Learning Disability*, 43(6), 515-529.

Lurae, C. and Johnson, H.C. (2008). Low Academic Performance and Specific Learning Disabilities. Retrieved from digitalcommons.liberty.edu/cgi/viewcontent.ch/article.

Madhuri, K., Sarika, K., Shubhangi, U., Sunil, K., and Sanjeev, A. (2001). Approaches to Learning Disability. *Indian Journal of Pediatrics*, 68(6), 539-546.

Malka, M., and Adi, S. (2002). The Mediating Role of Internet Connection, Virtual Friends, and Mood in Predicting Loneliness among Students with and without Learning Disabilities in Different Educational Environments. *Journal of Learning Disabilities*, 33(2), 82-87.

Margaret, S., and Margaret, S. (2010). Emotional Adjustment and School Functioning of Young Adolescents with Multiple versus Single. *Journal of Learning Disability*, 5(1), 109-112.

Michael, L.H., and Richard, M.M. (1998). Behavioural and Emotional Problems of Students with Learning Disabilities, Serious Emotional Disturbance, or Both Conditions. *Journal of Learning Disabilities*, 31(4), 327-338.

Michal Al-Yagon (2007). Socio Emotional and Behavioural Adjustment among School-Age Children with Learning Disabilities. *Journal of Special Education*, 40(4), 205-217.

Michal Al-Yagon (2011). Fathers' Coping Resources and Children's Socio Emotional Adjustment among Children with Learning Disabilities. *Journal of Learning Disabilities*, 44(6), 491-507.

Michal Al-Yagon and Mario, M., (2004). Socio Emotional and Academic Adjustment among Children with Learning Disorders. *Journal of Special Education*, 38(2), 111-123.

Michal, S. (2011). Knowledge about and Preoccupation with Reading Disabilities – A Delicate Balance. *Journal of Learning Disability*, 44(1), 80-93.

Michèle, M.M., and Myers, G.F. (2003). Complexities in Identifying and Defining Mathematics Learning Disability in the Primary School-age Years. *Journal of Learning Disabilities*, 53(1), 218-253.

Michels (2002). Parental Perceptions of the Affects of Learning Disabilities Assessment on Family Adaption. *Canadian Journal of Psychology*, 17(2), 15-29.

Miglani, P.P., Sandhu, P.K., and Kalra, D.S. (2011). Intelligence and need for Achievement Motivation of Children with Learning Disabilities. *Indian Journal of Psychology and Mental Health*, 5(2), 179-181.

Mishra, S.K., & Singh, R.D. (1998). Personality Adjustment of Graduates with Reference to their Socio-economic Status. *Praaachi Journal of Psycho Cultural Dimensions*, 14, 43-44.

Monroe, P. (1990). International Encyclopedia of Education. New Delhi: Cosmo Publications, 33-35.

Nancy, W., and James, M.L. (1998). The Effects of an Inclusive School Programme on Students with Mild and Severe Learning Disabilities. *Journal of Exceptional Children*, 64(3), 395-405.

National Institute for Literacy, 2006. Retrieved from https:/www.nichd.nih.gov/ publications/pubs/documents/NELPReport09.pdf.

National Institute of Child Health and Human Development, (2006). Retrieved from https://www.nichd.nih.gov/publications/pubs/documents/seccyd_06.pd

National Joint Committee on Learning Disability (1980). Retrieved from http://www.ldonline.org/about/partners/njcld

NIMH, (2001). Global Literature. Retrieved from www.ldac-acta.ca/learn-more/ld.../ understanding-learning-disabilities

No Child Left behind Act (2001). Retrieved from https://en.wikipedia.org/wiki/No Child Left Behind Act.

Pardini, P. (2002). The History of Special Education. Rethinking Schools, 16 (3).

Patnaik, N. (2011). Simultaneous and Successive Cognitive Processes in Normal and Disabled Children. *Indian Journal of Psychology and Mental Health*, 5(2), 200-203.

Paul, A., Weiseberg, R.P., Gcrare, J. and Nancy, L.L. (1990). A Comparison of Children with and without Learning Disabilities on Social Problems Solving Skill, School Behaviour and Family Backgrounds. *Journal of Learning Disabilities*, 23(2), 90-93.

Paul, T.S. (1995). Investigated on Full Inclusion of Students with Learning Disabilities and its Implications for Teacher Education. *Journal of Special Education*, 29(2), 234-244.

Pradhan, G.C. (1992). Values Pattern of School Students as a Function of Types of Schools and Levels of Intelligence. The Educational Review, 133-136.

Pradhan, G.C. (1993). Major Judgment of Secondary School Students as a Function of Types of School and Sex. The Educational Review, 64-67.

Raju, M.V.R., and Rahamtulla, K.T. (2007). Adjustment Problems among School Students. *Journal of the Indian Academy of Applied Psychology*, 33(1), 73-79.

Rebecca, S.M. and Margaret, S. (2004). Emotional Adjustment and School Functioning of Young Adolescents with Multiple Vs Single Learning Disabilities. *Journal of Learning Disabilities*, 37(5), 411-420.

Regina, S., and Scholte, E.M. (2012). Special needs Characteristics of Children with Emotional and Behavioural Disorders that Affect Inclusion in Regular Education. *Journal of Emotional and Behavioural Disorders*, 20(2), 92-104.

Renick, M.J., and Susan, H. (1989). Impact of Social Comparisons on the Developing Self-perceptions of Learning Disabled Students. *Journal of Educational Psychology*, 81(4), 631-638.

Rezique, J. (1983). Memory Deficits in Children with Learning Difficulties. *Journal of Learning Disability*, 27(3), 89-91.

Rogers, H. and Saklofske, D.H. (1985). Self-concepts, Locus of Control and Performance Expectations of Learning Disabled Children. *Journal of Learning Disabilities*, 18(5), 273-278.

Ron, N.J., Johnson, A. and Nancy, M. (2007). Effects of Direct Instruction, Cooperative Learning, and Independent Learning Practices on the Classroom Behaviour of Students with Behavioural Disorders – A Comparative Analysis. *Journal of Abnormal Psychology*, 5(2), 98-10.

Sakhuja, S. (2004). Education for all and Learning Disabilities in India. Retrieved from: URL:http://sspeonline.org/article.

Sater, G.M., and French, D.C. (1989). A Comparison of the Social Competencies of Learning Disabled and Low Achieving Elementary Aged Children. *Journal of Special Education*, 23(1), 29-42.

Shaffer, L.F. (1961). *Foundation of Psychology*, Edition 3, New York, John Wiley Publishers.

Shaonvaugh and Thompson, S.L. (2003). What is Special about Special Education for Students with Learning Disabilities. *Journal of Special Education*, 37(3), 140-147.

Sharan Vaughn and Janette (1998). Students' Perceptions of Inclusion and Resource Room Settings. *Journal of Special Education*, 32 (2), 79-88.

Sharma, N., and Gakkar, S.C. (1991). Adjustment of Students of Denominational Schools a Comparative Study. California, 3.

Sharon Vaughn and Elbaum, B.E. (1996). The Effects of Inclusion on the Social Functioning of Students with Learning Disabilities. *Journal of Learning Disabilities*, 29(6), 599-608.

Sharon Vaughn and Elbaum, B.E. (1998). Social Outcomes for Students with and without Learning Disabilities in Inclusive Classrooms. *Journal of Learning Disabilities*, 31(5), 428-436.

Sharon, O. (2010). A Struggle to Educate the Severely Disabled. The New York Times, 42-45.

Shaughnessy, T.E., and Swanson, H.L. (2000). A Comparison of Two Reading Intervention for Children with Reading Disabilities. *Journal of Learning Disability*, 33(3), 257-77.

Sheena, S., and Anamika, S. (2012). A Study of Different Aspects of Adjustment of Learning Disabled Children in Inclusive Settings. *An International Multidisciplinary Journal,* 1(4), 164-170.

Sheila (2010). Knowledge of Learning Disability among pre and in Service Teachers in India. *International Journal of Special Education,* 5(3), 132-138.

Shirley, A.S., and Milich, R. (1999). Social Persistence following Failure in Boys and Girls with Learning Disability. *Journal of Learning Disability,* 32(3), 201-212.

Simpson, R.L. and Sonja, R. (2009). Successful Inclusion for Students with Autism: Creating a Complete, Effective ASD Inclusion Program, 38-42.

Smith, C.R. (2004). Learning Disabilities the Interaction of Students and their Environments, Fifth Edition, Pearson Education, Inc. New York.

Smith, P. (2007). Have we made any Progress? Including Students with Intellectual Disabilities in Regular Education Classrooms. *Journal of Intellectual Disabilities,* 45(5), 297-309.

Stanley and Leonard (2001). The Reading and Writing Experiences of Children with Learning Disabilities. *Journal of Learning Disability,* 10(2), 17.

Status Canada, (2006). Retrieved from www.ldac-acta.ca/learn-more/ld-basics/prevalence-of-lds

Stephanie and David (1986). Social Competence and Behaviour Problems of Learning Disabled Boys Aged 6-11. *Journal of Learning Disability,* 19 (1), 39-45.

Stephen, C.L., and Robert. C. (1997). Interactions of First Grade Teachers with Learning Disordered Children. *Journal of Learning Disability,* 12(4), 20-25.

doi: 10.1177/002221949202500809 Stephenson, J., (1992). The Perspectives of Mothers whose Children are in Special day Classes for Learning Disabilities. *Journal of Learning Disability,* 25(8), 539-543.

Strawderman, C. and Watson, B.L. (1992). The Prevalence of Depressive Symptoms in Children with Learning Disabilities. *Journal of Learning Disability,* 25(4), 258-64.

Sunil, K., Rukshana, S., and Madhuri, K. (2011). Managing Specific Learning Disability in Schools in India. *Journal of Indian Pediatrics,* 48 (17), 515-520.

Sunita, B., and Manju, G. (2015). Role of Parental Involvement in Adjustments of Children with Learning Disability. *International Journal on Recent Trends in Life Science and Mathematics,* 2(2), 7-10.

Susan, A.V. (1990). Gender Differences in Intelligence, Language, Visual-motor Abilities, and Academic Achievement in Students with Learning Disabilities. *Journal of Learning Disabilities,* 23(1), 44-52.

Susan, H. (1998). Similarities and Differences in Domain-specific and Global Self-evaluations of Learning Disabled, Behaviourally Disordered, and Normally Achieving Adolescents. *Journal of Education*, 35(4), 653-680.

doi: 10.1177/082957359601100222 Symons, D., and Greene, C. (1996). Using Multiple Reporters of Problem Behaviour to Predict Clinical Referral of Adolescents with Learning Disabilities. *Canadian Journal of School Psychology*, 11(2), 178-190.

Tam and Swanson, L. (2000). A Comparison of Two Reading Interventions for Children with Reading Disabilities. *Journal of Learning Disability*, 33(3), 257-277.

Tanya, M.G., and Tanya, M.G. (2006). Social Cognition and its Relation to Psychosocial Adjustment in Children with Nonverbal Learning Disabilities. *Journal of Learning Disability*, 21(2), 35-37.

Tejeda-Delgado, M.(2009). Teacher Efficacy, Tolerance, Gender, and Years of Experience and Special Education Referrals. *International Journal of Special Education*, 24(1), 112-119.

The Child Mental Health Foundations and Agencies Network, (2000). Retrieved from www.researchconnections.org/childcare/ resourcesChild+Mental+Healt

Thomas, P.L., and Hunka, N.(2001). Teacher Education and Special Education - The Hournal of the Teacher Education Division of the Council for Exceptional Children. *Journal of Education*. 24(3), 183-197.

Thomas, P.M., and John, P. (1999). Building a model of Family care giving for Children with Emotional Disorders. *Journal of Abnormal Psychology*, 32(1), 16-19.

Thomas, W.F., and Philip, C.R.(1999).Teacher Assessed Behavioural Configurations, Peer-assessments and Self-concepts of Elementary Students with Mild Disabilities. *Journal of Special Education*, 33(2), 66-80.

Thorson, S. (2000). Macbeth in the Resource Room: Students with Learning Disabilities Study Shakespeare. *Journal of Learning Disabilities*, 28(9), 575-81.

Turnubull, A.P., and Ruief. (1997). Family Perspectives on Inclusive Life Style Issues for People with Problem Behaviour. *Journal of Exceptional Children*, 63 (2), 513-623.

U.S. Centers for Disease Control and Prevention, (2006). Retrieved from www.latimes.com › Topics › Health › Diseases and Illnesses.

UNESCO. (1995). Review of the Present Situation in Special Education. Retrieved from http://www.unesco.org/pv_obj_cache/ pv_obj_id_C133AD0AF05E62A C54C2DE8EE1C026DABFAF3000/ filename/281_79.pdf.

Vallance, B. (2001). Language Skills of Children with Emotional Behavioural Disorders. *Journal of Abnormal Psychology*, 10(1), 43-56.

Vaugghn, S. and Klingner, J.K. (1998). Using Collaborative Strategic Reading. *Journal of Exceptional Children*, 21(1), 36-38.

Vaughn, S., Elbaum, B.E., Shumm, J.S. & Hughes, M.T. (1998). Social Outcomes for Students with and without Learning Disabilities in Inclusive Classrooms. *Journal of Learning Disabilities*, 31(5), 428-436.

Vijayalakshmi, V.M., Viswanath, D.P., Nanasaheb, M.P. and Vital, M. (2011). Prevalence of Specific Learning Disabilities among Primary School Children in a South Indian City. *Indian Journal of Pediatrics*, 10(1), 23-25.

Virginia W.B., and Maggie, O.M. (2011). Evidence-based Diagnosis and Treatment for Specific Learning Disabilities involving Impairments in Written and/or Oral Language. *Journal of Learning Disabilities*, 44(2), 167-183.

Vogel, S.A. (1990). Gender Differences in Intelligence, Language, Visual Motor Abilities and Academic Achievement in Students with Learning Disabilities. *Journal of Learning Disability*, 23(1), 44-52.

Waggoner, H. and Lorraine, B. (1990). Concerns of Families of Children with Learning Disabilities. *Journal of Learning Disabilities*, 23(6), 386-390.

Warnock, R. (1978). Report of the Committee of Enquiry into the Education of Handicapped Children and Young People, London, 92-95.

Webber, J. and Scheuerman, B. (1993). Self Monitoring as a Behaviour Management Techniques in Special Education Classroom. *Journal of Special Education*, 14(2), 38-56.

Webber, J. and Brenda, S. (1993). Research on Self-monitoring as a Behaviour Management Technique in Special Education Classrooms. *Remedial and Special Education*, rse.sagepub.com14 (2), 38-56.

Wendy, B.H. (1990). The Self-perception of a Learning Disability and its Relationship to Academic Self-concept and Self-esteem. *Journal of Learning Disabilities*, 23(8), 472-475.

Williams, S.D. (2003). Factors Affecting Academic Achievement of Elementary Students in the Metropolitan Nashville Public Schools. *Journal of Learning Disabilities*, 29 (3), 234-238.

Wilson, L. (19750). Learning Disabilities as Related to Infrequent Punishment and Limited Participation in Delay of Reinforcement Tasks. *Journal of School Psychology*, 13, 255-263.

Wolffe, J. (2010). *What the Law Requires for Disabled Students*. The Oakland Press.

Index

S

❑ ❑ ❑ ❑ ❑